Managing Asperger Syndrome at College and University

A Resource for Students, Tutors and Support Services

Juliet Jamieson and Claire Jamieson

 **David Fulton** Publishers

David Fulton Publishers Ltd
The Chiswick Centre, 414 Chiswick High Road, London W4 5TF

www.fultonpublishers.co.uk
www.onestopeducation.co.uk

First published in Great Britain in 2004 by David Fulton Publishers
Reprinted 2006

10 9 8 7 6 5 4 3 2

Note: The right of Juliet Jamieson and Claire Jamieson to be identified as the authors of their work has been asserted by them in accordance with the Copyright, Designs and Patents Act 1988.

Copyright © Juliet Jamieson and Claire Jamieson 2004

British Library Cataloguing in Publication Data
A catalogue record for this book is available from the British Library.

David Fulton Publishers is a division of Granada Learning Limited, part of ITV plc.

ISBN 1 84312 183 2

Designed and typeset by Kenneth Burnley, Wirral, Cheshire
Printed and bound in Great Britain

Managing Asperger Syndrome
at College and University

Contents

Foreword

Asperger syndrome has increasingly captured the imagination of the general public. Many of us have marvelled at the fact that a person with Asperger syndrome may be highly intelligent, yet finds social interactions incredibly difficult; or is a great expert in a specialist field of knowledge, yet finds some of the simplest everyday tasks a challenge. This is cleverly illustrated in Mark Haddon's novel, *The Curious Incident of the Dog in the Night Time*, where Christopher has to act as a detective and models himself on Sherlock Holmes, who himself bears the traits of Asperger syndrome:

> The world is full of obvious things which nobody by any chance ever observes. But [Sherlock Holmes] notices them, like I do.

> [Sherlock Holmes's mind] . . . was busy in endeavouring to frame some scheme into which all these strange and apparently disconnected episodes could be fitted. (p. 92)

The irony is that Christopher does indeed notice strange things other people do not notice, yet he is unaware of the most obvious things that everyone around him already knows.

Let's imagine an older Christopher whose miraculous talent for maths would surely make him, sooner or later, a university student. He would undoubtedly not have problems with the difficult things such as lectures, seminars and exams, but would be baffled by the easy things, such as finding out about where to photocopy notes, who to sit with at lunch, how to deal with the laundry and where to get onto a course teaching study skills.

Juliet and Claire Jamieson have provided in this book just the sort of information about entering college and university that hardly anybody thinks of explaining to people with Asperger syndrome because they assume they know them already. In fact, many points that they write about are not well known at all, and while students can find out about them if they try, this is not always an easy task. So one expectation I have is that sisters and brothers of people with Asperger syndrome will turn to this book too when they go to university. Perhaps word of mouth will make sure that not only family members but also many other people can take advantage of the clearly set-out facts about transition from home to school, and about daily life as a student.

I am delighted that valuable information about Asperger syndrome, often in clear bullet-point format, is also included in this book for tutors, support staff and mentors in general. Special examination arrangements are discussed, as well as psychiatric problems and other conditions that appear to be associated with Asperger syndrome. A particularly useful section addresses the question of if and when it is appropriate to talk to others about Asperger syndrome and what disclosure might subsequently entail.

The authors of this handy collection of tips and information have provided a marvellous service. Just to learn about contact addresses, resources and support services is of tremendous value.

But there is much more: down-to-earth advice on dozens of everyday practical questions. The beauty is that these are questions one might not readily think of, and yet the answers can make a huge difference.

The high anxiety of the new should not be underestimated as it can, sadly, limit learning and adaptation. I hope that this user's guide to life at college or university will be a means to alleviate and prevent anxiety, and thus will, in no small way, contribute to a better life as a student.

UTA FRITH

Professor of Cognitive Development and
Deputy Director, UCL Institute of Cognitive Neuroscience, London

A Student's Perspective

In 1944, when Hans Asperger first described the syndrome which came to bear his name, he mentioned that one of his patients not only studied theoretical astronomy at university but also proved a mathematical error in Newton's work and went on to a promising academic career.

None the less, 60 years later, one of the biggest problems for further/higher education students with Asperger syndrome (and other autistic spectrum conditions) is their invisibility.

For the last seven years, I have run an email support group for college and university students with AS and high-functioning autism. I have seen many of the issues described in *Managing Asperger Syndrome at College and University* recur again and again, while struggling with them myself as an undergraduate and postgraduate student.

Although awareness of AS is increasing rapidly, some people (like me) still don't receive an accurate diagnosis until after they leave school. Even when a student arrives with a diagnosis, they may well find that the institution is unfamiliar with AS and unprepared (or even unwilling) to adjust.

Often staff find it hard to appreciate that it is possible to have the intellectual and verbal skills necessary for academic work, while still experiencing the social and sensory differences that characterise the autistic spectrum. In many cases, disability services in tertiary education are oriented towards students who have physical disabilities or specific learning disabilities. They may be entirely non-plussed by a student whose needs don't fit that framework.

College or university can provide an invaluable, semi-supported environment in which people with AS can develop independence while focusing on our areas of academic interest. But it can also pose particular challenges. Without the structures of school or home, students can feel as if we have been thrown in at the deep end – to swim, or sink.

If we're lucky, we may find individual staff members who are willing to provide guidance and mentoring; if we're not, we may be left to flounder (I ended up dropping out of postgraduate work largely as a result of miscommunication with a tutor).

This book is thoughtful, positive, and never patronising. My only regret is that it wasn't available when I first started university. Its clear presentation of a wealth of practical information and insightful recommendations would have saved me from enormous amounts of stress. As it is, I will certainly be keeping a copy to hand when I return to university in September.

CLARE SAINSBURY

Author of *Martian in the Playground: Understanding the Schoolchild with Asperger's Syndrome* (Lucky Duck Publishing) and founder of University Students with Autism and Asperger's Syndrome website and list

Preface

Asperger syndrome is a pervasive developmental disorder within the autism spectrum, the manifestations of which change over time, depending on the particular demands placed on the individual. This resource focuses on the difficulties encountered at university and college by those with Asperger syndrome, including the critical period of transition from school, living away from home, personal organisation, social pressures and academic issues. Potential problems and pitfalls are explored and possible solutions and coping strategies are suggested.

The diagnosis of Asperger syndrome has become prevalent only in the last 10 to 15 years. Children are often diagnosed at about seven years of age, and it therefore follows that many students with diagnosed Asperger syndrome are now entering colleges and universities.

Although there have been numerous research studies about this condition, and there are many excellent publications giving guidance to parents and teachers, the focus of attention to date has been largely on children rather than young adults.

As a result of recent legislation (the Disability Discrimination Act 1995), institutions of higher education are obliged to take account of any disabilities students may have, and to make 'reasonable adjustments' to ensure that they receive fair treatment. There is considerable expertise within the disability services of many colleges and universities about dyslexia, sensory impairment and physical disabilities. However, it is now important that the needs of students with autism spectrum disorders are recognised so that disability coordinators and assessors can make appropriate provision for them.

The purpose of this book is to offer information, support and advice to students with Asperger syndrome, their parents, their peers and staff, both academic and pastoral. Potential problems are identified in a range of social and academic contexts, and practical strategies and solutions are proposed. Students with Asperger syndrome are much more likely to be able to cope with their living arrangements and social life, and to complete their degree courses successfully if they have been able to access appropriate guidance and support.

Included with this book is a CD of various resources for use either by the students themselves, their mentors or other support staff. These include advance information for interview panels, an information leaflet about Asperger syndrome for academic staff, a suggested initial interview form for the use of support staff, and templates for a mentoring record form, for personalised information to be given to academic staff and for a weekly timetable.

Acknowledgements

We would like to thank Ellis Meade for his willingness to talk in depth about the effects of his Asperger syndrome, giving us an insight we would never otherwise have had, and the other undergraduate and postgraduate students at University College London (UCL) and elsewhere who talked to us; Marion Hingston Lamb, the Disability Coordinator at UCL, and Jenny O'Sullivan, the Disability Support Officer, who have worked with us for the last year setting up a support service for students with Asperger syndrome, an exciting new initiative for us all.

We would also like to thank Juliet's colleagues at the Child Development Centre in Stevenage: Consultant Community Paediatricians Dominic Croft, Margit Bommen and Kemi Adejare, with whom she has worked over the last nine years in the field of autism spectrum disorders in children and adolescents. They have been generous with their professional knowledge and expertise, which has been invaluable in writing this book. Thanks too are due to Iain Harris, who has taken a great interest in this project.

People with Asperger syndrome are remarkable in their ability to learn to adapt and compensate for their difficulties. They can achieve the highest levels of education and a successful professional career.

Uta Frith, 2003

1

Asperger Syndrome

This chapter provides an introduction to the aspects of Asperger syndrome that will most concern readers of this book. The main focus is on the problems and challenges faced by people with this condition, and helping them to understand the adjustments they need to make when they move from school to college or university.

What is Asperger syndrome?

Asperger syndrome is an autism spectrum disorder. It was first described by an Austrian psychiatrist, Hans Asperger, in 1944 in his paper, 'Autistic Psychopathy in Childhood', but it was some 40 years before information about the condition began to be widely disseminated in the fields of education and psychology.

Asperger described four boys who had a 'fundamental disturbance in common' resulting in severe difficulties with social integration. Often the boys' social problems were so profound that they dominated their lives. Asperger stated that in some cases a 'high level of original thought and experience' compensated for social problems. He also stressed that people with these social difficulties can 'fulfil their social role within the community especially if they find understanding, love and guidance'. Although Asperger did not relate autistic psychopathy to intelligence in 1944, in a later paper (1979) he recorded his observation that children with 'infantile autism' had a propensity to high intelligence with special abilities in areas of logic and abstraction.

Dr Lorna Wing (1981) was the first person to use the term 'Asperger's syndrome' to describe 34 individuals whose profile resembled that of the four boys described by Asperger in 1944. She concluded that an individual could be autistic and yet still have considerable abilities in language, cognitive skills and social interest. Since Uta Frith's English translation of Asperger's original study was published (Frith 1991) the condition has become increasingly recognised in the English-speaking world. Recent scientific and media attention has now brought Asperger syndrome into the wider public domain.

Asperger syndrome is characterised by the presence of three major functional impairments, in the absence of general learning difficulties. These impairments occur in:

- social interaction and social relationships
- verbal and non-verbal communication
- imagination, behaviour and flexibility of thought.

There continues to be some confusion about the terminology used to describe individuals with autistic features who have superficially good language skills and average or above-average cognitive abilities. Throughout this book the term 'Asperger syndrome' will be used, rather than terms which are often used synonymously, such as high-functioning autism, autistic continuum disorder, autism spectrum disorder, atypical autism and mild autism. Using the label 'mild' to describe an autistic disorder significantly understates the severity of the problems encountered by people with Asperger syndrome and their families, who do not consider their disorder to be mild in any way.

Hans Asperger stressed the developmental characteristics of the syndrome he described; as individuals grow older and mature, their profile of strengths and difficulties changes. Strategies and support systems that were appropriate at a particular stage of development, for example at primary school, will need to be monitored, evaluated and adjusted on an on-going basis as the child passes from adolescence to adulthood.

Asperger strongly believed that the children he studied had the potential to grow up to be successful in their working lives and to make a positive contribution to society. He was convinced that their future success was dependent on appropriate education and support based on a thorough knowledge of their strengths and weaknesses.

> 'I like the way I think for the most part, and the fact that I have Asperger syndrome doesn't bother me – I am happy that I can see many things that so-called "normal people" can't see. I won't be able to forget about having Asperger's – ever. It's me and that's it.' *EM*

Diagnosis of Asperger syndrome

A key aspect of the diagnosis of Asperger syndrome is that, while there are diagnostic criteria, there is no single formal diagnostic process. Members of different professions have developed an interest in Asperger syndrome, including paediatricians, psychologists, psychiatrists, speech and language therapists and specialist teachers. Many of these people may consider that they have sufficient expertise to make a diagnosis. There are as yet no regulations as to the professional qualifications required to make a diagnosis. This means that informed individuals may suspect the syndrome and make an informal diagnosis without seeking professional advice or confirmation.

A diagnosis of Asperger syndrome is rarely made before a child is five years old, and the syndrome is more frequently identified after a child has been at school for a few years. Children who are eventually diagnosed may previously have been thought of as different in some way, for example autistic, hyperactive or presenting with unusual behaviours.

There has been a significant increase in the diagnosis of Asperger syndrome in recent years. The incidence of the syndrome is unlikely to have changed but greater public and professional awareness, including clearer diagnostic criteria and tools, has had this effect. The current consensus is that Asperger syndrome affects approximately 1 in 250 of the population, with a ratio of six males to one female (Gillberg 2002).

Hans Asperger did not suggest formal diagnostic criteria. Lorna Wing (1988) described the syndrome and its various manifestations in detail but she did not lay down specific criteria for diagnosis either. It was only 15 years ago that Gillberg and Gillberg (1989) set out specific diagnostic criteria, focusing on six categories of impairment. According to Gillberg (1991), five out of the six impairments need to be present to make a definitive diagnosis. (See Box 1.)

These six categories are sub-divided into twenty specific symptoms listed in Box 1, of which at least at least nine have to be present for a positive diagnosis.

Box 1

1. Social impairment (extreme egocentricity)	**At least two of the following:** (a) difficulties interacting with peers (b) indifference to peer contacts (c) difficulty interpreting social cues (d) socially and emotionally inappropriate behaviour
2. Narrow interest	**At least one of the following:** (a) exclusion of other activities (b) repetitive adherence (c) more rote than meaning
3. Compulsive need for introducing routines and interests	**At least one of the following:** (a) routines and interests which affect every aspect of everyday life (b) routines and interests which affect others
4. Speech and language peculiarities	**At least three of the following:** (a) delayed speech development (b) superficially perfect expressive language (c) formal pedantic language (d) odd prosody, peculiar voice characteristics (e) impairment of comprehension including misinterpretation of literal/implied meanings
5. Non-verbal communication problems	**At least one of the following:** (a) limited use of gestures (b) clumsy/gauche body language (c) limited facial expression (d) inappropriate facial expression (e) peculiar, stiff gaze
6. Motor clumsiness	Poor performance in a neurodevelopmental test

Diagnostic criteria for Asperger syndrome first appeared in the International Classification of Diseases and Disorders (ICD-10) published by the World Health Organisation in 1993 (WHO 1993). The following year the disorder was included in the Diagnostic and Statistical Manual (DSM-IV) (American Psychiatric Association 1994).

Both the ICD-10 and the DSM-IV specified that a diagnosis of Asperger syndrome could only be made if the criteria for autism were *not* met. The ICD-10 also emphasised the significance of a history of normal language and social development in the first three years of life. However, in a clinical setting it is unusual for children presenting with Asperger syndrome to have had unremarkable cognitive, linguistic and social development in these early years. They are likely to have developed language skills which may appear extremely advanced, but the type of language and their social use of this language are frequently unusual. For example, the ability to recite large sections of dialogue from a favourite video such as *Thomas the Tank Engine*, with perfectly replicated words, accents and intonation patterns, does not necessarily indicate an ability to engage in functional conversation. Speech is often described as being pedantic and quaint, with little awareness of a conversational partner.

Some people for whom a diagnosis of Asperger syndrome would be appropriate may not meet all the diagnostic criteria, as individual personality traits and cognitive strengths and weaknesses may distort the clinical picture. There is also thought to be some variation in the clinical profile according to gender. Gillberg reports that in his experience

> . . . girls with Asperger syndrome are sometimes less aggressive, less prone to hyper-activity and are not so fixated on specific narrow interests. They tend to be more interested in 'social' toys, such as dolls, whereas boys often demonstrate a stronger interest for hard objects, water, sand and mechanical things. (Gillberg 2002)

It may also be particularly difficult to differentiate Asperger syndrome from some other developmental disorders, such as autism and attention deficit hyperactivity disorder (ADHD). It is possible that hyperactivity and impulsiveness camouflage some of the social difficulties encountered in Asperger syndrome; however, when the hyperactivity is treated with medication, the social problems become more apparent.

Genetic studies have revealed that many people diagnosed with an autism spectrum disorder have close relatives who exhibit some manifestations of Asperger syndrome without meeting the full diagnostic criteria. Personality traits such as eccentricity, social withdrawal, preoccupying interests and obsessions are often identified in the extended family. This is often referred to as the broader phenotype (or lesser variant) of autism.

> 'It was a huge relief when I was finally diagnosed with Asperger syndrome. I had known all my life that I was different and couldn't relate to other people but I didn't understand why I was so different.' *EM*

With increasing media exposure and the availability of books and articles about Asperger syndrome readily available, many adults are now being diagnosed for the first time. As most specialists in Asperger syndrome work with children, it can be difficult to obtain a diagnosis as an adult. However, the National Autistic Society's Centre for Social Communication Disorders (established in 1991) will provide assessments and diagnoses for children, adolescents and adults. The Centre accepts referrals for children and adults of all ages and all levels of ability. The assessment includes the administration of a semi-structured interview called the Diagnostic Interview for Social Communication Disorders (DISCO), developed by Drs Lorna Wing and Judith Gould. (For information about this centre and other centres for diagnosis, see the contact addresses on p. 93.)

> 'There is a danger of reading too much about Asperger syndrome and then subconsciously taking on the characteristics described in books about the syndrome.' *JA*

An Asperger syndrome profile

Although people with Asperger syndrome share some behavioural characteristics, they are as different from one another in personality, aptitude and attitudes as are all other individuals. There is a risk, when a diagnosis is made, that people may be identified by their syndrome without their individuality being recognised. This can lead to prejudice and stereotyping, which may exacerbate feelings of isolation experienced by people with Asperger syndrome.

Any attempt to outline a typical Asperger syndrome profile should therefore be interpreted with caution. With that in mind, recognised manifestations of Asperger syndrome are described below.

Most of the features described are recognised behaviours, present in the wider population to varying degrees. They are only considered significant and distinguishable from standard behaviours when they appear in combination, and to such an extent that everyday functioning is affected. For example, people generally have a strong desire to follow familiar routines such as sitting in the same place on a train or meeting room, but when this is not possible they are not unduly concerned. For people with Asperger syndrome, however, such situations can cause anxiety and distress, which can sometimes lead to extreme emotional reactions.

Impairments in social interaction and social relationships

Poor social understanding

Difficulty in understanding social conventions or codes of conduct and a lack of awareness of the conversational partner can lead people with Asperger syndrome to dominate conversations or to talk in what seems to others an inappropriate or tactless way.

> 'I often don't realise if I have said something rude or tactless, which can make me look heartless or insensitive.' *JA*

> 'Even when people point out to me that I have said something tactless I can't always see what they mean.' *EC*

Poor non-verbal communication

Limited eye contact and an inability to pick up non-verbal cues from others can make people with Asperger syndrome appear insensitive to the hidden social messages that form part of every interaction. Successful communication depends on conveying more information than the verbal message alone. People with Asperger syndrome may not notice whether conversational partners are bored, want to change the subject, make a contribution or bring the conversation to a close. These messages are normally communicated subtly and non-verbally, through, for example, touch, facial expression, tone of voice, gesture and body posture.

> 'People sometimes say they get tired of hearing me talking about the same thing over and over again but it is difficult for me to know what else to talk about.' *EC*

Difficulties in engaging reciprocally in group activities

Many young people with Asperger syndrome find it very difficult to work collaboratively. This is due to the high levels of social awareness required for groups to work together successfully. People with Asperger syndrome may have a tendency either to dominate or to withdraw from a group, and they are likely to feel generally uncomfortable with group dynamics. This obviously has implications for students working in seminar, tutorial or study groups.

> 'I really don't like having to work in a group when I feel I do much better work on my own.' *EM*

Difficulty fitting in with the interests and activities of peers

Many people with Asperger syndrome do not share an interest in the current trends, fashions or hobbies followed by their peer group. This may be because they have their own special interests

> 'I couldn't see why anyone in their right minds would want to spend their evenings having conversations with drunk people in the overheated and crowded college bar.' *Clare Sainsbury*

that preoccupy and absorb them or simply because they are immune to peer pressure and to the urge to follow the crowd.

Limited or unusual facial expression and eye contact

The facial expression of people with Asperger syndrome frequently fails to conform to expected norms, and this can have a significant effect on social interaction. Some people may stare intently at their conversation partner, making them feel uncomfortable (this might be the result of over-correcting a previous lack of eye contact). Others may find it very difficult to make any eye contact at all during a conversation. Some adults have reported that they find it difficult to look at someone and listen at the same time. A 'dead pan' facial expression is not unusual and this again interferes with conversational flow, as partners have difficulty interpreting feelings or emotions when the facial expression is so inscrutable.

> 'I find it difficult to look at people when I am talking to them because I get very distracted by small details I notice on their faces and then I lose my train of thought.'
> *MC*

Christopher Gillberg has made the following observation:

> Very typical is the 'dead face', 'stone face' or depressed look, followed by the big smile, indeed sometimes laughter, as soon as a conversation comes to an end (as though from relief that there will be no further requirement for interaction). This latter symptom often remains one of the hallmarks of the syndrome in adult age. (Gillberg 2002)

Easy target for bullying or manipulation by others

A history of bullying, social isolation, indifference or manipulation by others is a feature at some time in the lives of most people with Asperger syndrome. The overt bullying sometimes experienced during adolescence often becomes more subtle in later years; however, it can still be a very negative and painful experience. Often individuals are unaware that they are the victims of bullying, cruelty or indifference because they have difficulty understanding other people's behaviour in general. It is important that people with Asperger syndrome are aware of their potential vulnerability and that any incidences are identified and addressed to minimise their damaging consequences.

> 'Indifference is probably a more effective form of bullying than overt bullying.'
> *EM*

Difficulty in making friends

An awareness that other people appear to have effortless friendships, relationships and social lives only serves to increase feelings of social isolation and loneliness. Undoubtedly some people will be quite content with their own company and interests, but more often there is a strong desire to make friends and, as a result, a tendency to treat the most casual encounters with people as potential friendships. This can be followed by feelings of disappointment and rejection when there is no further contact following a first meeting.

> 'I felt that half of me wanted to socialise, but that the other half wanted to withdraw and continue along a linear learning path without the intervention of other people.'
> *EM*

Social isolation and loneliness

The loneliness experienced by many people with Asperger syndrome can lead to poor self-esteem and even mental health problems such as depression and anxiety.

> 'My mobile phone never rang and gathered dust behind my computer. Consequently, I withdrew.' *EM*

> 'I feel as though I have two mindsets – I watch people interacting with each other in sunny garden squares, and I constantly think about those people and why I don't have the skills that they seemingly take for granted.' *EM*

Impairments in verbal and non-verbal communication

Literal interpretation of language

People with Asperger syndrome tend to interpret language literally. For example, if someone is standing by a closed door holding a heavy pile of books and they say, 'Can you open the door?', the appropriate response would be to open the door for them. The literal interpretation would simply be to answer 'Yes' without inferring the implied meaning. Ambiguous sentences may also be misinterpreted because of a failure to take account of context. For example, a boy with Asperger syndrome was waiting at a bus stop with his mother and she asked, 'Shall we go upstairs on the bus?' To her surprise he replied, 'Don't be silly; buses can't go upstairs.' It is surprising how many utterances can be construed as ambiguous in this way. Similar problems also arise in the understanding of idioms (you drive me round the bend/keep your eyes peeled), metaphors (she was a raging bull/he is a gentle giant) and other figures of speech. Jokes, particularly puns, teasing and sarcasm ('Oh brilliant, it's raining!' and 'That's really helpful!') may also be taken literally and misinterpreted.

> 'I don't always realise when people are making jokes or teasing each other and it makes me think that they are being rude or unkind.' *MC*

> 'I find abstract concepts difficult despite the fact that my "problem" is abstract.' EM

Pedantic speech style

A tendency to use formal and unabbreviated language with an extensive vocabulary can make speech appear very longwinded and, at times, even pompous or pretentious. The idioms and slang words that feature widely in other students' conversations may be conspicuously absent from the speech of a student with Asperger syndrome.

Monotonous tone of voice and odd or inappropriate intonation

Changes in tone, volume and intonation are important features that add to the meaning of spoken language. The speech of people with Asperger syndrome often appears to lack variation in intonation, stress and rhythm, which can give their speech a monotonous quality. It is not unusual for them to be good mimics of others' accents or to have the ability to repeat dialogue from a film or television programme, accurately reproducing the original intonation and stress patterns. However, when this is followed by spontaneous speech the

> 'Sometimes my pitch was normal, at other times it was deep like I was doing an Elvis impersonation. When I was excited it sounded like Mickey Mouse after being run over by a steam roller – high-pitched and flat.' *Donna Williams*

quality often reverts to a monotone. Particular moods or situations may cause people with Asperger syndrome to speak in a particularly high or low voice, or with an exaggerated intonation pattern.

Echolalia and palilalia

Echolalia is repetition of other people's words and phrases, either immediately after hearing them or at a later time (delayed echolalia); palilalia is repetition of one's own words. These features are seen at an early developmental stage in childhood but occasionally persist into adulthood. Palilalia is more commonly seen with individuals who have developed signs of Tourette syndrome in addition to Asperger syndrome.

Limited ability to describe own and others' feelings or emotions

Although people with Asperger syndrome may be able to speak fluently, and use well-developed language structures when they are talking about something that holds a particular fascination for them, they are not usually able to express or discuss emotions with the same facility.

> 'I know exactly how I am feeling but when someone asks me I don't know what to say.' *TH*

> 'I can see when I have upset people, but when they confront me, I usually take it out on those people because I'm in denial about what I have done wrong to upset them.' *JA*

Tendency to dominate conversations

Many individuals with Asperger syndrome have an intense, obsessional special interest, sometimes obscure (e.g., scaffolding, radio antennae), sometimes very ordinary (e.g., computers). They are inclined to talk about these special interests at every opportunity, paying little regard to whether the topic is appropriate for the situation or whether others are interested. (See 'Special interests' below.)

> 'I can only speak for myself when I say that if one subject is on my mind or I am fascinated by something, then literally everything else is insignificant.' *Luke Jackson*

Tendency to be argumentative and inflexible

Many parents and teachers are aware that it can be unwise to disagree with, or get into an argument with people with Asperger syndrome. They are often extremely persistent and continue to reiterate their point of view long after the debate would appear to have run its normal course. A combination of not being able to let go and a strong conviction that they are right seems to fuel such behaviour.

> 'I always seemed to be getting into arguments with people in the department and I got very angry. Later I realised that I had been arguing over something silly just for the sake of it.' *JA*

> 'I stand my ground when people try to open me up to new ideas or challenge me about my ideas. I feel as though these people are attacking me when they try and make me aware of things that I do wrong.' *EC*

Impairments in imagination, behaviour and flexibility of thought

Strong adherence to rituals and routines

People with Asperger syndrome have a strong need for order and predictability, which leads them to develop rituals and routines which they adhere to rigidly. They have a fear of the chaos which might ensue if there were any forced change in the aspects of their lives that they feel they can control. There is evidence to show that at times of anxiety, transition or instability, insistence on routine becomes more dominant and elaborate (Attwood 1998).

Special interests, collections and obsessions

Special interests often appear to dominate the lives of people with Asperger syndrome. Thomas the Tank Engine, trains, dinosaurs or space are generally common interests in childhood, but for people with Asperger syndrome the interest becomes all-consuming, dominating conversations and precluding other activities.

People with Asperger syndrome may also develop a fascination for more unusual subjects, such as lawnmowers, maps or radio antennae, and may be surprised when others do not appear to share their enthusiasm. Collecting, categorising and lining things up are ways of maintaining structure, order and predictability, which can be reassuring and comforting when so many other things in life appear to be unpredictable and disorganised. Any objects that are easily available can form a collection; for example, stones, pieces of string, crayons, cars or stamps. Facts such as dates and scores of sports events, bus or train routes, capital cities or world records are frequently learned, memorised and recited to others. Interests may suddenly be dropped, and something that once held a strong fascination may lose its appeal, to be replaced by a new curiosity.

> 'Batteries are very good to hold. They are cool and smooth and fit perfectly into your hand . . . Another reason why I like to collect batteries was purely and simply that I liked collecting. In a disorganised world is there anything more satisfying than organising your possessions? I think that is why people line things up.' *Luke Jackson*

Resistance to change

Resistance to change in daily routine or environment is often apparent in early childhood. This is another way of maintaining order and predictability in an unpredictable world. If something has been done in a particular way, or a certain route has been taken, it is reassuring for these things to be repeated in exactly the same way time after time. This insistence on 'sameness' was observed by Hans Asperger as a pattern of elaborate repetitive routines. There are many implications of this inflexibility for students, who can be thrown by sudden changes to their timetables, teaching staff or venues. Once they feel comfortable attending a lecture, given by a known lecturer, knowing that each week they will sit in the same seat in the lecture theatre, it can cause extreme distress if one of these variables is altered. Following rules or patterns leads to predictability but when, as often happens, these are adapted, changed or even disregarded by those in control, students with Asperger syndrome may feel inordinately upset.

> 'Rules were – and are – great friends of mine. I like rules. They set the record straight and keep it that way. You know where you stand with rules and you know how to act with rules. Trouble is, rules change and if they do not people break them. I get terribly annoyed when either happens.' *Lianne Holliday Willey*

Imposition of rituals

The imposition of rituals on oneself or on others can be a driving force in some people with Asperger syndrome. There may be a need to think particular thoughts at particular times or to perform prescribed actions. These rituals can develop around everyday activities such as meal times, getting dressed or going to bed. The desire for sameness mentioned above feeds these rituals, which can interfere with normal functioning not only for the person with Asperger syndrome, but for others drawn into the ritual. Rituals often involve performing certain actions or behaviours before beginning an activity, for example, putting things in an exact place around the bedroom before getting into bed. When this behaviour becomes extreme, interfering seriously with everyday life, it can be considered a form of obsessive compulsive disorder (see p. 72).

Confusion or fear induced by new events or situations

The need for predictability and familiarity makes adapting to new situations and circumstances difficult for people with Asperger syndrome.

Impaired ability to empathise

People with Asperger syndrome have difficulty imagining how another person thinks and feels, which is a cognitive function described in the literature as 'Theory of Mind'. This includes understanding that other people have different knowledge, beliefs and desires from one's own. Theory of mind begins to emerge in young children from the age of about 18 months and continues to develop throughout childhood. Children on the autism spectrum are remarkable in their lack of this ability to read, or show any interest in other people's thoughts. They frequently show little interest in performing activities that need the participation or cooperation of someone else. Uta Frith suggests that people with Asperger syndrome who have difficulties in this area 'are able to learn slowly, and those with sufficient verbal ability are able to develop an explicit theory of mind' (Frith 2003). However, people with Asperger syndrome do not have a natural propensity to empathise.

Lack of motivation

People with Asperger syndrome may lack motivation for engaging in activities and subjects that are not related to their special interests, especially if the reason for the activity is not clear. This is evident in the reluctance of students with Asperger syndrome to complete assignments that do not interest them or that seem irrelevant.

> 'I sometimes find that the lecture title doesn't seem to reflect the subject matter of the course or that the lecturer doesn't seem to make sense when he is explaining something. I often lose interest and can't be bothered to listen any more.'
> *EC*

Poor attention levels

Attention and motivation are strongly linked – lack of interest leads to lack of motivation, which in turn leads to reduced attention. In many people with Asperger syndrome there are additional problems with attention control. Occasionally attention problems are linked to absorption in a chosen activity which is so all-consuming that they find it difficult to focus on anything else. This absorption may take the form or day-dreaming or appearing to be in 'another world' where there is little awareness of anything else happening in the immediate environment. At other times attention may be affected by extreme distractibility; seemingly insignificant factors such as sounds, lights, smells or textures cannot be ignored and consequently become the focus of attention.

Difficulty generalising skills

Once a particular skill, social act or behaviour has been learned in a specific situation it is not always easy for people with Asperger syndrome to apply this knowledge to different circumstances.

Inability to deceive or understand deception in others

The fact that most people with Asperger syndrome are inclined to tell the truth can cause them some difficulties. For example, they may not realise that some sensitive information should be kept confidential. They may give relative strangers too much information about themselves, such as their address or telephone number. They may also be inclined to take others' honesty for granted; for example they might not be aware of the risk of entrusting belongings to a stranger for safe keeping.

Unusual responses to sensory stimuli

Hypersensitivity to sound, visual stimuli (particularly lights and colours), textures, tastes, smells, movement, pain and temperature are commonly observed in people on the autism spectrum. There is evidence to suggest that about 40 per cent of young people with Asperger syndrome have some abnormality of sensory sensitivity (Rimland 1990). One or, occasionally, more than one of the senses is acutely sensitive to stimuli, which can cause extreme anxiety and distress. It is not uncommon for children to cover their ears or eyes in an attempt to exclude sights or sounds that they find overwhelming in their intensity. These sounds might be as commonplace as a vacuum cleaner motor, the ringing of a telephone, applause or a doorbell, but perception of them can be unbearably intense. For many children this hypersensitivity reduces with maturity, but it can continue to be a problem for some individuals throughout their lives. Sometimes ordinary background noise, such as an electrical hum or the sounds from lifts or escalators, can become so intrusive that concentration is affected, to the extent that it is impossible to carry on a conversation.

Visual hypersensitivity is less common than sensitivity to sounds. However, some people are equally distracted and unsettled by lights and colours, particularly fluorescent lighting strips that flicker, bright sunlight that reflects on shiny surfaces and illuminates tiny dust particles, or even dark shadows that distort visual perception.

Sensitivity to the taste and texture of food is again a common feature of childhood that often diminishes in adolescence and adult life. Some people may continue to have an aversion to certain foods, however, or to have a strong desire to eat the same foods with the same textures every day of their lives.

In some people reaction to touch and extreme sensitivity to tactile stimuli can cause difficulties. This may relate to sensory defensiveness in different parts of the body or to an intensity of sensation from different textures, fabrics or materials.

Perfectionism

Perfectionism, leading to constant dissatisfaction with, for example, the standard of their work, is a problem for some adults with Asperger syndrome. A fear of failure and a determination to achieve the perfect piece of work can make progress very slow and arduous. Perfectionism may be confined to certain areas and disregarded in others. For example, part of the bedroom where there are objects of special significance may be well ordered and structured while the rest of the room is untidy. Perfectionism can be a positive attribute, particularly for processing precise and exact technical or scientific data.

Narrow focus of interest

People with Asperger syndrome are often fascinated with intricate details or small parts of objects rather than perceiving objects as a whole. For example, they may be extremely good at completing complex jigsaw puzzles, sometimes even upside down, but they may show little interest in the end result.

High levels of anxiety

Anxiety can lead to poor concentration, under-achievement and low self-esteem, and can have implications for mental health. This area is covered in detail in Chapter 7, 'Secondary and Associated Problems'.

Poor motor coordination

Weakness in motor skills, including clumsiness, unusual or stiff gait and illegible handwriting is a feature of Asperger syndrome. Paradoxically, people who appear to be clumsy can be dextrous and proficient when they are engaged in an activity that holds a fascination, for example model-making or fine art. Digby Tantum (1991) states that 'Clumsiness may not be entirely attributable to motor abnormality. It is, for example, a feature of the self-consciousness of adolescents who are striving to adopt new and more socially acceptable motor schemata.'

Inappropriate or gauche body language

Many individuals have poor awareness of the conventions of personal space when they are talking to other people; they may either stand too close or stand too far away, making it difficult to conduct a conversation.

> 'I am told that I sit too close to people and follow them around unnecessarily . . . apparently I go too close to everyone . . . If you stand too close to a member of your own sex, then you will be called gay, and if you stand to close to the opposite sex, everyone will say that you fancy them.' *Luke Jackson*

Stereotypical and repetitive body movements

Movements such as hand flapping or wringing, body rocking or spinning are diagnostically significant features of Asperger syndrome in childhood. These movements often become less frequent or even disappear with maturity. Occasionally these mannerisms re-emerge at times of extreme stress in adult life, when they are likely to take a less noticeable form, for example finger tapping or flicking.

Difficulty recognising people

Face recognition is often difficult for people with Asperger syndrome. They may have no trouble recognising a lecturer in the lecture theatre but would not recognise the same person in an unfamiliar context, for example in a shop.

Strengths

The features outlined above all relate to problems and difficulties experienced by people with Asperger syndrome. To redress the balance it is important to emphasise the many strengths and positive qualities that arise as a result of the condition. Many of the characteristics of people with Asperger syndrome relate to an excessive interest in objects and systems rather than people or relationships, which can be advantageous in certain circumstances. Individuals may have some or many of the strengths listed below. Acknowledging these assets will help people with Asperger syndrome to understand that, although they might be different from many of their contemporaries, their differences can be both productive and valuable. This recognition can significantly increase confidence and self-esteem, making it possible to compensate for difficulties and, consequently, to achieve and succeed. It is important that any mentoring or support for people with Asperger syndrome should emphasise and make use of individuals' particular interests and learning styles rather than simply focusing on the aspects of their characters that cause them problems.

Average or above-average intellectual capacity

'Intelligence Quotient (IQ) is probably higher in a group of people with Asperger syndrome than in the population at large' (Gillberg 2002). Hans Asperger suggested that there could be a correlation between the incidence of Asperger syndrome and highly intelligent or gifted parents. Cognitive ability is probably the greatest asset for people with this condition and it should be acknowledged and emphasised.

Wide vocabulary

People with Asperger syndrome may acquire a wide vocabulary related to subjects that have a special fascination for them. This may have been a feature from early childhood, and a wide vocabulary might have developed over the years, reflecting the different topics of interest that have been read about and studied.

Savant abilities

Some people with Asperger syndrome have an exceptional talent or skill. These special abilities may be in almost any field, including drawing, painting, music, calendar calculation or feats of rote memory.

Good visual and spatial skills

Many people with Asperger syndrome would describe themselves as 'visual learners'. They are able to take account of visually presented detail and to perform tasks which demand excellent awareness of the size and shape of objects.

Excellent long-term, rote or photographic memory skills

People with Asperger syndrome are often able to remember a huge amount of detailed information, often related to their special interests.

Aptitude for acquiring system-based knowledge

An ability to acquire system-based knowledge, such as computer programming and mathematics, and an ability to identify and absorb patterns in data such as dates, shapes, timetables, number strings or number plates are recognised strengths for many people with Asperger syndrome.

Extensive knowledge of specialist subjects

The knowledge that is accumulated through special interests may, depending on the subject matter, be highly valued in an academic environment.

Relative immunity to peer pressure

A person with Asperger syndrome 'follows own desires and beliefs rather than paying attention to or being influenced by, others' desires or beliefs' (Baron-Cohen, Leslie and Frith 1985). An ability to resist 'following the crowd' is an advantage in many situations.

Hyperlexia

People with Asperger syndrome are often precocious in their development of reading skills. They are able to decode text very accurately, but they may have difficulty with certain aspects of comprehension.

Honesty and loyalty

A natural propensity to tell the truth can sometimes result in apparent insensitivity and tactlessness. People with Asperger syndrome do not generally tell 'little white lies' to avoid hurting people's feelings or to shield them from an unpalatable truth. But they are often steadfastly loyal to people who have been understanding and supportive. Honesty and loyalty are valued attributes in relationships and society.

Sense of humour

People with Asperger syndrome often have an idiosyncratic sense of humour; they are often amused by absurdity, black humour or observations they have made about the mannerisms or behaviour of others.

Insight into the nature of their difficulties

People with Asperger syndrome are often analytical about the way they feel and behave and the way in which they differ from others, particularly in the way they react in social situations. This insight plays a vital role in any counselling or social skills training and, together with motivation, helps to make adaptation and change possible.

> 'I will struggle on despite the fact that I have a huge "problem", I am very determined.' *EM*

Willingness to accept support

Young adults who have a diagnosis of Asperger syndrome are often very willing to accept support. They tend to be conscious of the things they find challenging and difficult, and consequently are willing to negotiate their way through problems and accept advice if this is clearly rationalised. Many show persistence and determination to come to terms with and, where possible, to overcome their difficulties.

Synaesthesia

Synaesthesia is an involuntary sensory experience in which the actual information received by one sense is accompanied by a perception in another sense. For example, certain words are strongly associated with specific colours, tastes or smells, so that every time a particular word is heard, a corresponding colour, taste or smell is evoked. Synaesthesia is a relatively rare condition in the general population but it is thought to be more prevalent in people with Asperger syndrome (Harrison and Baron-Cohen 1995). People who experience this condition find it very difficult to imagine that other people do not have similar sensations. Experiencing senses in another mode can greatly enhance artistic or musical creativity and can provide the basis for excellent memory strategies.

> 'I have a rich ability to relate sounds and smells to images and to relate music and sounds to whole experiences. This enables me to establish connections that other people perhaps cannot appreciate.'
> *EM*

Perfect pitch

It has been observed (Sacks 1995) that more people with Asperger syndrome than in the general population have perfect pitch. That is, they are able to identify the musical pitch of a note they hear as, for example, B flat, or to sing a note at will or on demand at a particular pitch, without the support of a musical instrument. Although the advantage of perfect pitch for musicians cannot be underestimated, those with this gift have difficulty tolerating musical performances that fall below their exacting standards.

Key points from Chapter 1

- The identification and diagnosis of Asperger syndrome has increased dramatically in recent years

- A range of professionals may be involved in diagnosis

- Students with Asperger syndrome are vulnerable because of their problems with social interaction and communication

- Students with Asperger syndrome are individuals who should not be 'pigeon-holed' as a result of prejudice

- The strengths of students with Asperger syndrome should not be overlooked

- Appropriate support can greatly improve students' experience at college and university

2

Statutory Rights and Support

The Special Educational Needs and Disability Act 2001

The Special Educational Needs and Disability Act 2001 (SENDA) protects students enrolled on educational courses from discrimination as a result of their disability. The Act came into force on 1 September 2002, from which time institutions needed to make 'reasonable adjustments' in order to provide appropriate support for students with disabilities. Since September 2003 there has also been an obligation to provide 'auxiliary aids and services' for disabled students, and from September 2005 all buildings in educational establishments should have been adapted to make them accessible and usable for people with disabilities.

The Act applies to all students attending educational courses run by 'responsible bodies', including sixth form colleges and further and higher education establishments. Student services covered by the Act include a wide range of educational and non-educational services, such as assessments, short courses, field trips, exams and arrangements for work placements.

The Act states that, 'It will be unlawful for responsible bodies to treat a disabled person "less favourably" than a non-disabled person for a reason that relates to the person's disability.' If for any reason a disabled person is at a 'substantial disadvantage', responsible bodies are required to take reasonable steps to prevent that disadvantage. These steps might include:

* changes to policies and practices
* changes to course requirements or work placements
* the provision of support workers
* the delivery of the course in alternative ways.

The law requires that educational establishments anticipate the requirements of disabled students and that appropriate provision and reasonable adjustments are made. This can be done through regular staff reviews, staff training and reviews of practice.

Disabled Students' Allowance

Disabled Students' Allowances (DSA) are grants from public funds that are available to students with disabilities who are attending a higher education course (including degree courses run by the Open University or other distance learning establishments). Students who have been awarded the DSA while studying for a first degree can reapply if they subsequently study for further degrees, as they may have additional or different needs. The allowance does not apply to students in further education.

The DSA provides for the extra costs of services, provisions and facilities that students may need to complete their studies successfully. In most cases it is awarded by the student's Local Education Authority (LEA), but when degree courses are funded by the National Health Service or research bodies it is these institutions that fund the DSA.

The DSA (2003–4) provides for the following allowances.

Specialist equipment allowance

This is a one-off payment of, currently, up to £4,355 for the time it takes to complete a programme of study leading to a first degree (or undergraduate level qualification). This could cover the funding of equipment such as computers, specialist software, mini disks, tape recorders, technical support and equipment insurance premiums.

Non-medical helpers' allowance

This is an annual payment of up to £11,015 for students in full-time study. This could be used to fund mentoring, additional support services and specialist counselling.

General allowance

This is an annual payment of up to £1,090 for students in full-time study, to cover miscellaneous expenses such as additional photocopying, printer cartridges and audio tapes.

The DSA is not means tested and there are no age restrictions, neither does receipt of the allowance affect the payment of any state benefits. It is intended purely to cover the expenses incurred participating in higher education courses.

Eligibility

Students are eligible for the DSA if they have:

- residential status in the United Kingdom
- no outstanding loans from the Student Loans Company
- a disability, specific learning difficulty, a mental health difficulty or a medical condition that will require support and incur extra costs
- evidence of a disability such as a doctor's letter, medical certificate or diagnostic assessment by a qualified individual or organisation.

Evidence of entitlement to disability state benefits such as Disability Living Allowance or Incapacity Benefit are not normally accepted as evidence of disability.

Course results do not affect the DSA for the following year even if it is necessary to repeat or change to another course. However, if the course is abandoned in the early stages it may be necessary to make repayments. It is possible to take a break from studies and reclaim the DSA on their resumption.

Assessment of need

Those eligible for a DSA should contact their LEA or funding body to ask for the contact details of the DSA student support officer. They will then be asked to send in a diagnostic assessment report or other appropriate evidence that they have Asperger syndrome. The next step is a referral to an Access Centre for an Assessment of Need.

The assessment at the Access Centre takes the form of a personal interview with an assessor, who will take a full case history and discuss needs and support requirements in the context of students' particular courses of study. The assessment results in a detailed report, with clear recommendations regarding specialist equipment or technology and non-medical support, such as mentoring and tuition in study skills. All recommended equipment and support is itemised and purchase prices are included. Access Centres can give advice about any technical equipment and software that may be recommended, and training in the use of recommended software is usually funded through the DSA.

Following the Assessment of Need, a 'Profile and Learning Contract' is drawn up, and with the student's agreement this information is copied to the relevant academic, administrative and pastoral staff, ensuring that any recommendations and advice are known and hopefully implemented. The report is sent to the student and to the LEA or funding body. LEAs then contact students to let them know how to access the allowance. Procedures vary from one funding body to another.

If students' circumstances change during the course a reassessment may be indicated. Any equipment provided by the DSA becomes the personal property of the student and does not need to be relinquished at the end of the course, unless the award has been granted when the student is about to complete the course.

The Learning Contract remains valid for the duration of the course, although it can be revised, amended or updated should circumstances change.

The procedure for awarding the DSA is slightly different in Scotland. More information can be obtained from the Student Awards Agency for Scotland (SAAS). See Contact Addresses, p. 93.

Accessing support at college and university

Once students have settled into their college or university one of the first things they should do is to make contact with the Disability Support Staff. It is possible that students will have already made contact with this service at some time during the application procedure and they may have already spoken to or met some of the staff.

There are a number of benefits for students with Asperger syndrome in arranging an early meeting with the disability staff:

1. To make sure that they are on the register of students with disabilities.
   If the student declared their diagnosis of Asperger syndrome on their college or UCAS application form they should find that their name is already on the register of students with disabilities. If they have not done so they can register when they visit the Disability Office. If they are not registered they may not be able to access the support and advice that the disability service can offer.
2. To obtain information about the disability service.
   Students will need to know about opening hours, accessibility of staff, appointment systems and the most appropriate method of contacting the service if concerns or problems arise. Email or written communication is often preferable to telephoning or visiting the office as this can be disruptive or intrusive.
3. To find out how to go through the process of applying for the Disabled Students' Allowance. The disability staff will be able to guide students through this procedure, which varies to some extent from one LEA to another.
4. To arrange for Access Centre recommendations in the Assessment of Need to be put in place.

This might include advice to academic or residential staff, mentoring, student counselling, befriending, buddy systems, Health Centre services or perhaps meeting others known to the service who also have Asperger syndrome.

5. To find out about any special facilities.

Some institutions have facilities for the sole use of disabled students. These might include quiet areas, or computer cluster rooms with special software.

6. To arrange for appropriate outside agencies to meet any recommendations that come beyond the remit of the college or university.

Contact may need to be made with psychologists, therapists, mentoring services or local or national support services for adults with Asperger syndrome, such as the National Autistic Society.

7. To agree to advice and information being given to the student's teaching staff and those responsible for administering examinations.

This would include any special arrangements that need to be made regarding teaching methods, use of technical support and exam arrangements.

8. To give students the opportunity to voice any specific concerns they have about settling in to their new life at college or university.

Student counselling

Many students experience problems that they are unable to manage without some outside support. Students with Asperger syndrome are even more likely to encounter emotional and psychological difficulties than their peers, and may need to make use of the student counselling service in addition to any support they are receiving for problems directly related to their disability. Most colleges and universities have trained counsellors who offer a service to any students who are having difficulty coping with some aspect of their personal lives. This service is totally confidential and any information that is given during the counselling sessions will not be divulged without the student's prior consent. Appointments with a student counsellor can usually be arranged at short notice.

Counselling may be given in groups or on a one-to-one basis. Individual counselling is usually given in blocks of five to six hourly sessions once a week. Many different emotional or psychological problems can be addressed:

- crisis management for an immediate problem such as assault, theft or abuse
- relationships
- sex or sexuality
- alcohol and drug-related problems
- eating disorders
- stress and anxiety
- depression
- self-injury or suicidal thoughts
- bereavement
- parental separation or divorce
- homesickness
- anger management.

Student counselling services often provide handouts and suggested reading material for coping with particular problems, and can refer students to other professionals when appropriate. Many institutions offer a drop-in service where appointments are not required, and students can be seen for a short session on a first-come first-served basis.

The role of a mentor

The word 'mentor' comes from the Greek word meaning 'enduring', and is defined as a sustained relationship between a youth and an adult. Through regular contact the adult offers support, guidance and advice to the younger person who is experiencing a difficult time in their life. Many colleges and universities run their own mentoring service and it can be very helpful for students with Asperger syndrome to make use of this provision. In practice, the mentor may be someone near the student's own age who has been given specialist training. Anyone taking on the role of a mentor needs to have specialist knowledge of the student's disability and should be prepared to make a firm commitment. The aim of this kind of support is to help young people with Asperger syndrome to develop an insight into and understanding of their own specific strengths and weaknesses and how these facets of their personality affect their lives and the lives of the people around them.

Mentors for students with Asperger syndrome may take on different responsibilities, for example:

- natural mentoring or befriending – based on friendship, teaching, coaching and counselling
- structured or planned mentoring – a more formal process that follows a structured programme
- educational and academic mentoring – strategies are developed to cope with difficulties with course work, individual study or exam preparation
- personal development mentoring – providing support at times of stress or when making difficult decisions.

A proficient mentor will probably take on a combination of these roles. The following guidelines are suggested as a basis for effective mentoring.

Information gathering

A detailed individual profile of the student ideally should be obtained before a programme of mentoring can be planned. (See 'Initial Interview' in the Resource section of the book, p. 84.) It may take up to two mentoring sessions to go through the structured interview, but this is an effective means of exploring the ways in which the student is most likely to benefit from mentoring. The information gathered can be used as the basis for a confidential report or advice sheet (see p. 87) which may, with the student's consent, be given to support, academic or residential staff.

Practical arrangements

The arrangements for the date, length, venue and frequency of the mentoring sessions need to be agreed and recognised as a commitment. Any changes to the arrangements should only be made by the mentor if they are unavoidable, as breaks in the routine could make the student feel anxious and insecure, thus undermining the reassuring nature of the sessions.

Students may want or need more frequent and longer mentoring sessions at the beginning of the contact, and once some issues are resolved the sessions may become less frequent.

Record keeping

It can be helpful for the mentor to make notes at each meeting so that issues that arise can be addressed in subsequent sessions (a sample form is given in the Resource section on p. 85). Records might include the following:

- general discussion (issues that have arisen since the previous session)
- specific experiences and events that have been either positive or negative
- whether anything can be learnt from these experiences
- any specific strategies, changes or adaptations that can be implemented to learn and generalise from these events
- specific targets for the following week or weeks until the next meeting
- other issues or topics discussed
- date, time and venue for the next session.

The record forms provide a structure for the sessions and can be kept to monitor development and progress throughout the mentoring process.

Liaison

The mentor's role may include liaison with members of college or university staff, or may even involve acting as an advocate for the student if required. Advice can be given to the Disability Support Staff and other staff about the specific needs of the student in terms of social issues, teaching delivery, assessment and examinations.

Range of focus

Mentoring can provide support for different needs, including academic, practical (financial, living arrangements, transport) and social.

Fostering independence

Problems of dependency can arise between students and their mentors. For this reason the roles need to be clearly defined and contact should normally be limited to pre-arranged appointments. The long-term objective for successful mentoring is to enable students to develop coping strategies so that they can function with decreasing levels of support over time.

Key points from Chapter 2

- Students with Asperger syndrome are protected in law from discrimination under the Disability Discrimination Act

- Institutions' Disability Services will be able to help students to access the support they need

- UK students with written evidence of a diagnosis of Asperger syndrome are eligible for the Disabled Students' Allowance

- Funding may be provided for technological support and personal assistance.

- Students who are experiencing emotional or psychological problems may find their institution's counselling service helpful

- Increasingly, institutions are training mentors to work with students with Asperger syndrome

3

Transition from School to College

Career advice is given to all pupils at school from the age of 14, to help them decide whether they will leave school at 16 and go to college to study a vocational course, take an apprenticeship or enter the job market, or whether they will continue their studies on to AS and A level at school or at a sixth form college.

Pupils with a recognised diagnosis of Asperger syndrome also need their future education to be considered and planned from the age of 14 (Year 9). Young people with a diagnosis are themselves involved in the Year 9 annual review where reference is made to the transition plan: crossing the boundary between school and the early stages of life as an adult.

> 'I was coping with leaving home and the shock of a new environment in my own way, retreating into my college room (occasionally retreating under my desk) until gradually I felt safe and at home there and could venture out to explore.'
> *Clare Sainsbury*

Local Education Authorities must inform the designated officer in the Social Services department about any pupils attending their schools who have a diagnosis of Asperger syndrome. Social Services are legally required to provide plans for children with significant special needs including provision for further education.

The Connexions Service

The Connexions Service provides personal advisers who give specialist advice to all young people aged between 13 and 19 about choosing subjects and mapping out future educational and career plans. They also provide a nationwide service for children with additional or special educational needs between these ages. They have a very accessible website – www.connexionsdirect.com – and pupils can contact an adviser by telephone, web chat, email or text messaging. Their employees offer confidential and practical advice about a wide range of issues that affect young people and they have a special interest in supporting those with Asperger syndrome and other special needs. If they are unable to answer specific queries they will be able to refer students to someone with more specialist knowledge. (See Contact Addresses, p. 93.)

Leaving school

The annual review in Year 11, when the pupil has reached school-leaving age, provides an important planning opportunity for those pupils who are leaving school after their GCSE exams. For pupils continuing their education at a local regional college it is very helpful if links can be made between present and future staff. In this way support strategies can be maintained or modified to suit the new educational setting.

The Local Education Authorities (England and Wales), the Students Awards Agency for Scotland (SAAS), the Northern Ireland Education and Library Board and the Channel Islands or Isle of Man Agency are responsible for making appropriate provision for young people until they reach the age of 19. For those pupils who continue their education to A level and then wish to apply for higher education courses, the transition period will begin at the time they make their application to college or university (usually in the Autumn term before they take their A levels), and will continue throughout that year until they register for their new course the following September or October.

There are a number of good practices that can be put in place to ease the transition from school to college or university for people with Asperger syndrome.

Developing staff awareness

1. Information about Asperger syndrome can be made available for all college and university staff who have contact with students: lecturers, tutors, learning support staff, student counsellors, residential wardens, students' union representatives, housekeepers and canteen staff.
2. A named person from the school can be involved with the transition stage. This facilitator should have the opportunity to liaise with the student, parents and future support staff.
3. More specific and detailed training about Asperger syndrome can be made available for student counsellors, learning support staff, disability staff and mentors who are offering direct support to students. (See Box 2.)

Training should cover:

- the effect of Asperger syndrome on studying and learning
- the effect of the syndrome on social skills
- support services such as counselling, mentoring or befriending
- giving advice on strategies for coping with stressful situations
- setting up a 'withdrawal policy' including the identification of quiet areas where students can go for solitude or relaxation
- developing awareness of problems that students may encounter during the course, such as aversion to change, organisational difficulties, social isolation and anxiety
- provision of support at critical periods throughout the course when there is a change to the normal routine, such as syllabus alterations, changes to assignment deadlines, field trips, exam periods, study leave, reading weeks, changing from one year to the next and vacations
- giving support at the end of the course to facilitate transition to further study or entry into the workplace.

Initiatives students can take

1. Students with Asperger syndrome can compile a list of useful questions they would like to ask about colleges or universities when they attend open days.
2. Students can visit their new college or university during the summer holidays. Their visit will enable them to become familiar with the site and facilities. If possible, arrangements should be made for them to meet key members of staff, such as the disability coordinator and their personal tutor.
3. Information about the institution and course, from the prospectus and from correspondence

sent out in the summer vacation, can be studied before the beginning of term. This usually includes maps of the site and local amenities, a detailed timetable of where and when the student needs to be in the first few days of term, and contact details for relevant members of staff.

4. The Disabled Students' Allowance application can be made in advance so that support needs have been assessed and identified before the beginning of term. (See section on the DSA, p. 17.)

Some organisations in the UK, such as the National Autistic Society, InterACT Centre, London, ESPA (European Services for People with Autism) in Newcastle, and the College of Nautical Studies, Glasgow, offer advice to other institutions about good practice for students with Asperger syndrome. (See Contact Addresses for details, p. 93.)

The experiences of school leavers with Asperger syndrome are very variable. Some will have had negative experiences including bullying, isolation and even exclusion. Others may have had a more successful time at school, particularly if they have received appropriate support and guidance throughout their education. The manifestations of Asperger syndrome are varied and extensive, each individual being affected in different ways depending on factors such as personality, interests, ability and experience. It is important to take these factors into account when making plans for higher education.

Gap year

Many students choose to take a gap year between school and university. Others may follow an apprenticeship or find employment straight from school and then decide to return to full- or part-time education as a mature student. For all students, gap years need to be well planned and structured. Students with Asperger syndrome in particular need to know exactly how they are going to spend a gap year, as they could be vulnerable during this period if there is too much free time and lack of routine. Useful information about gap year activities can be found on websites listed in the Contact Addresses and Resources section of the book (p. 93).

A gap year might also be an ideal opportunity for students to take the time out from formal education to concentrate on developing skills, perhaps through counselling, training courses or workshops, which will benefit them as young adults. Courses are available to develop confidence and assertiveness, on anger management, social skills and relaxation techniques. The National Autistic Society runs a number of these throughout the country and also holds information about courses run by other organisations. There are also increasing opportunities for individuals to work on social skills using the virtual environment of the Internet; 'Aspiechat' (see list of websites, p. 98) allows multiple users to develop social interaction in a virtual environment, which has the advantage of enhancing confidence without the stress of face-to-face contact. Health centres, GP surgeries and health clubs can give advice and contact details about local services and courses available for relaxation, such as the Alexander Technique, yoga, meditation and general stress management.

Where to live

Students attending their local college or university, or one that is within easy commuting distance, will have the option of continuing to live at home. Growing numbers of students are now choosing to live at home while at university for financial reasons. Staying at home can seem appealing for people with Asperger syndrome because they have the chance to participate in student life but with the security of maintaining familiar living arrangements.

There are, however, potential disadvantages in staying at home. It is more difficult to develop an independent lifestyle with a certain amount of privacy within the confines of the family home. Parents may, understandably, find it difficult to acknowledge that students need more freedom at this stage of their lives, and may continue to treat them in exactly the same way as they did when they were at school. Although moving away from home can be a difficult time for all students, it is likely to be particularly challenging for those with Asperger syndrome because of the enforced change to all aspects of their routine. However, if the appropriate support and advice is in place, this could be the ideal time to make the transition to living more independently.

Courses

Students can feel overwhelmed by the vast range of available courses and the responsibility for making an appropriate choice.

There are three main types of courses:

1. Vocational courses, such as General National Vocational Qualifications or National Vocational Qualifications (GNVQs or NVQs).
2. Academic courses, such as physics, chemistry, philosophy, English literature, languages or classics.
3. Professional training at degree level, such as medicine, nursing or physiotherapy.

Many young people with Asperger syndrome choose to leave school at the age of 16 when compulsory education finishes. Local and regional colleges offer a wide range of vocational courses that train students for employment in specific fields, such as catering, hairdressing, motor vehicle maintenance, plumbing, etc.

As most people with Asperger syndrome develop special interests in particular subjects, their resulting expertise can often be developed through following a related vocational course.

National Vocational Qualifications (NVQs)

NVQs are available at five levels, and courses leading to these qualifications are followed by individuals from the age of 16 onwards. In the last ten years around 300 NVQ courses have been developed. Some of these are offered at colleges throughout the country but others may only be found at specialist centres. Many people studying for NVQs are also working in full- or part-time jobs.

General National Vocational Qualifications (GNVQs)

From the early 1990s many colleges and schools have offered their students the opportunity to complete a programme of vocational education, in parallel with AS and A levels, designed especially for the 16 to 19 age range. There are three levels of GNVQ: Foundation level (equivalent to four GCSEs at Grades D–G), Intermediate level (equivalent to four or five GCSEs at Grades A–C) and Advanced level (equivalent to two A levels). GNVQ units are designed to cover a broad range of knowledge related to a chosen subject. The courses have three Core Skills Units: Communication Skills (English), Application of Number (Maths) and Information Technology (Computer skills). GNVQs are offered in a number of different subjects. The following should be available at most regional colleges and many secondary schools and sixth form colleges:

- Art and Design
- Business
- Construction and the Built Environment
- Engineering
- Health and Social Care
- Information Technology
- Leisure and Tourism
- Management Studies (Advanced level only)
- Media: Communication and Production (not Foundation level)
- Performing Arts and Entertainment
- Retail and Distributive Services (not Foundation level)
- Science.

In additional to NVQs and GNVQs there are also a number of institutions that offer vocational qualifications such as the City and Guilds of London Institute (CGLI), Oxford Cambridge & RSA (OCR) examination board,) and the Business & Technology Education Council (BTEC).

Youth Training Schemes (YTS)

These are designed to prepare young people who have left school after Year 11 (at 16 or 17) for employment. Students on youth training schemes study for NVQs at levels 1, 2 and 3. The schemes vary across the country as they are administered by 81 different Training and Enterprise Councils (TECs). They are run by employers who try to encourage local young people to embark on training that meets the needs of the local community and who will hopefully provide later employment opportunities. Youth Credits, ranging from £750 to £5,000, are available in the form of a voucher that can be used to fund training through the TEC-approved agencies.

Modern apprenticeships

Modern apprentices involve young school leavers in training as they work.

Levels 1, 2 and 3 of an NVQ are completed as the apprentice demonstrates competence in a range of skills, which is usually assessed by the employer.

Degree courses

These are offered at universities and colleges. They are becoming more widely available and one school leaver in three now continues into higher education. A degree course of at least three years is a big commitment and requires dedication and staying power. Approximately 15 per cent of students drop out of their degree course and leave university early each year. The most common reason students give for leaving is that they made the wrong choice of course.

There are many different types of courses, including:

- *single subject degrees* – one subject is studied in depth, with or without a subsidiary subject
- *joint degrees* – two subjects are studied simultaneously, both to a similar level; they are often related subjects, such as English and Linguistics, but they can be from entirely different disciplines
- *combined degrees* – a number of subjects are studied, some in more depth than others
- *modular degrees* – modules are taken throughout the course until enough have been passed to obtain a degree; this allows for some flexibility between different institutions
- *interdisciplinary degrees* – broad-based studies related to a particular theme, such as Urban Studies, Environmental Science, Human Sciences or Architectural Studies
- *sandwich courses* – involving placements in industry or commerce, either in short blocks or with a whole year spent in a placement
- *degrees with a licence to practise in a particular profession* – often related to medicine and include medicine itself, dentistry, physiotherapy and speech and language therapy
- *foundation courses* – offered by many universities for students whose qualifications do not meet the standard entry requirements for degree courses. On the successful completion of a foundation year in a particular subject, students can then transfer to a degree course in a related subject.

The best reference guide for undergraduate admission is the official publication from the Universities and Colleges Admissions Service (UCAS). UCAS also produces a magazine *University and College Entrance* (UCAN), which should be available through schools, colleges, careers offices and public libraries. This is a useful publication which gives details of different institutions, the courses they offer and the admissions and entry requirements. More advice can be found in the UCAS book *Guide to Higher Education*.

When choosing a college or university course it is worth considering degrees that have a natural career progression, such as accountancy, architecture, law or computer programming. Students with Asperger syndrome also need to consider whether particular career paths might be inappropriate for them because of the stress they might induce, or the fact that communication skills and teamwork are essential attributes for the job.

Choice of college or university

One of the first things to do when considering further or higher education is to try to narrow down a very wide choice. There are over 320 universities and colleges throughout the UK, offering over 50,000 full-time higher education courses.

There will be a number of considerations when choosing a college or university. Deciding on a location will quickly narrow down the options. If it is desirable to live at home the choice will be limited to the available places within a reasonable commuting distance. If that is not a restriction it may be advisable to choose a location that can be reached by car or public transport without too much difficulty or expense. The geographical situation may also be important; most universities are in large towns and cities but some are in more rural settings which might be preferable for those who wish to pursue countryside interests. The choice of courses, the type of accommodation available, whether the university has a campus or city centre site, and the pastoral and support services offered are all factors that will influence students in deciding on their shortlist for applications.

Distance learning

Enrolling on a distance learning degree course is a good option for some people with Asperger syndrome, particularly if they are anxious about changing their lifestyle or are apprehensive about moving away from their home environment. Individuals with particularly strong computer skills may also find distance learning suitable. Much of the tuition is given through a computer conferencing system, allowing students to study from home with links to databases. Television and radio are also used in the teaching process and tutors keep in touch with students through email.

Distance learning courses will usually involve attending occasional tutorials at both day and residential schools. This is an opportunity to meet people studying the same subject in a highly structured environment. In recent years there has been a significant rise in the number of students under the age of 25 who are choosing to study with the Open University. The Open University was founded in 1970. It had its origins in the National Extension College (NEC), which was a project designed to create educational opportunities in the wider community by providing distance learning courses.

Students taking distance learning degree courses are eligible for the Disabled Students' Allowance.

The advantages of distance learning for people with Asperger syndrome include:

- studying in their home environment
- combining studying with employment
- avoiding getting into debt
- using computers and information technology for learning
- providing the opportunity to meet and socialise with others at day and residential schools while staying at home for most of the course
- receiving support from a personal tutor
- the possibility of taking home-based exams.

Prospectuses

Prospectuses are issued by colleges and universities each year, usually in April or May. Institutions also display their prospectus information on the Internet. Copies of some prospectuses may be available at schools and colleges but it is often necessary to contact the institutions directly to request the current publication.

The prospectus gives detailed information about the facilities, including accommodation, methods of teaching, welfare and recreation, and type and content of the courses on offer. The entry requirements for individual courses are usually stated, both for post-A level entry or entry as a mature student through the Access route. There is no point in considering courses unless there is a realistic expectation of meeting the entry requirement. There should also be a section in the prospectus covering the facilities and provision made for students with special needs and disabilities. There may be contact details for the Disability Officer, who would be able to provide more detailed information about the services available for people with Asperger syndrome.

For mature students hoping to enter into higher education, or for those without suitable qualifications, UCAS offers Access courses in a number of different subject areas all over the UK. These are usually held in further education colleges and can be taken on a part-time basis. Most courses are completed in one year and their results, which are assessed through coursework and examinations, are recognised by the QAA (the Quality Assurance for Higher Education) as qualifications for university entry. Access courses act as preparation for students who lack the educational criteria needed for higher education, and therefore, as well as the relevant academic studies, each course contains a 'core element' of study skills to enable students to cope with the demands of university life.

Open Days

It is very helpful to make use of institutions' open days, as they provide an opportunity to find out about different courses and teaching methods. Some institutions arrange for prospective applicants to attend a lecture and to visit the library and the halls of residence during the open day. It may also be possible to arrange an individual visit by contacting the admissions department. Most colleges and universities will be prepared to arrange private visits for prospective students with special needs, if they are given notice. A visit provides an opportunity to get more specific information about the different options for living arrangements and accessing any support services. It could also be a good opportunity to meet and talk to undergraduates at the college who have Asperger syndrome and who are happy to share their experiences. The Disability Coordinator is likely to be able to organise this if requested. UCAS publishes a handbook listing all the open days. Regional Colleges of Further Education, sixth form staff and the Connexions service (see p. 93) provide information about regional colleges and the courses they offer.

The application process

Applications for vocational and non-degree undergraduate courses are handled directly by the individual colleges. Each institution has its own application forms and admission procedures. Similarly all postgraduate and research posts are handled by individual universities. All application forms have a section where applicants can give details about any disability or special needs. Although Asperger syndrome might not be mentioned as one of the examples of a disability, it is strongly recommended that this information is provided at the application stage. Disclosure enables the college to make appropriate arrangements to support the student through the admissions and interview processes and throughout their course.

UCAS – The Universities and Colleges Admissions Service

The UCAS system handles applications for approximately 200 different institutions that offer degree, DipHE and HND courses. The Open University and many colleges of art, drama and music have their own application procedures and need to be contacted directly.

There are three different ways of making a UCAS application:

1. **apply** – UCAS's web-based application system (www.ucas.com)
2. EAS – the Electronic Application System, CD-based
3. paper application form.

The UCAS form can be obtained from the student's school or college or directly from UCAS (see Contact Addresses, p. 96). The form has an accompanying handbook which should be read carefully. As the application form is updated and changed from year to year it is important to check that a current one has been provided.

Students can choose to apply to between one and six different institutions, except for Medicine, Dentistry and Veterinary Medicine/Science, where the maximum number is four. There is a standard application fee of £15 for two to six choices and £5 for a single choice.

There are three important deadlines that must not be missed:

- 15 October – deadline for applications to Oxford and Cambridge and for courses in Medicine, Dentistry and Veterinary Medicine/Science
- 15 January – deadline for all other applications except Art and Design
- 24 March – deadline for Art and Design.

There are advantages in making an electronic application; the software is able to check for errors and students have the opportunity to alter and update the form. It is very important to double-check the codes for the institutions and the codes for the individual courses.

Disclosure

Section 2 of the UCAS application form relates to 'Further Details', where there is a box to tick for those with a 'Disability/special needs (including dyslexia)/medical condition'; applicants with Asperger syndrome should mark this box. Section 8 of the form gives a small space for the applicant to detail any 'Special needs or support required because you have a disability or medical condition stated in Section 2'. The current code for people with an autism spectrum disorder or Asperger syndrome is T. This disclosure enables the university or college to make appropriate provision for planning support and assistance for the student's time as an undergraduate. If applicants do not want to disclose their disabilities at the time of filling in their form it is possible to leave this section blank.

Personal statement

The personal statement helps the colleges and universities to choose between candidates who have similar academic records. This is the opportunity to give reasons why you want to study a particular subject and to give personal information about achievements and interests. It is essential to have some practice runs at the personal statement and to ask a teacher or a trusted adult to check it carefully before submitting the final draft with the application form. As part of the personal statement some students may feel the need to disclose the fact that they have a diagnosis of Asperger syndrome because it is clearly an integral part of their personal identity. This is a good opportunity to focus on the strengths that are associated with the condition rather than emphasising problems or weaknesses.

Interviews

Some universities choose to interview applicants for certain subjects. Interviews can be very stressful for people with Asperger syndrome. It might make the student feel more confident about the experience if they are able to send advance information to the interview panel explaining about Asperger syndrome and how the condition could affect their performance during an interview (see Resources, p. 93). In particular it might be helpful at this point to stress difficulties with social interaction:

- variable eye contact (too much or too little)
- unusual body posture
- unusual tone or volume of voice
- literal interpretation of language
- difficulty addressing more than one person on the panel
- tendency to talk too much or too little
- difficulty changing from one topic to another
- assuming the interview panel has prior knowledge
- difficulty interpreting non-verbal communication
- difficulty anticipating when the interview is coming to an end.

Offers

For students sitting A level examinations colleges and universities usually make conditional offers of places on courses, in which they specify the examination grades that need to be achieved. Students who have already taken A levels or who have already met the entry requirements are given unconditional offers. If an offer is not made, the institution does not have to give any reasons for its decision. If students are worried that their performance at interview might have let them down, they will sometimes be offered feedback if they contact the admissions tutor.

It is not necessary to respond to any offers until decisions have been received from all the institutions, although a conditional or unconditional offer can be accepted at any time. UCAS will eventually request a formal response, when the appropriate box on the form needs to be completed. Any institutions that have rejected an application, or where the prospective student has withdrawn their application, will be marked X. The other boxes should be marked by the student.

It is at this point that students who have been offered several places need to reject all but two of these. They need to decide which is to be their first choice, and which they will keep in reserve in case they do not achieve the required grades at A level. Students with unconditional offers will not need a reserve choice.

The boxes should be marked as follows:

- **F** for a Firm acceptance (first choice)
- **I** for Insurance (reserve choice, usually requiring lower grades)
- **D** for Decline (all other offers).

The deadline for completing the form will be stipulated by UCAS and varies from year to year; it is important that this deadline is met. Accepting an unconditional offer, or an offer where you go on to meet the conditions of that offer, is contractually binding.

Students holding conditional offers should contact their chosen universities as soon as they know their A level results. If the exact requirements are not met there is the possibility that the institution will still offer a place. For those who do not fulfil the specified requirements and who are refused both their conditional offers, it is possible to go into the Clearing schemes, whereby institutions fill their available places. Immediately after the A level results are released the daily newspapers publish information about vacancies, and prospective students need to contact the colleges or universities where their application will be considered.

Key points from Chapter 3

- The annual review in Years 9 and 11 of secondary school is a good opportunity to address the future plans of pupils with Asperger syndrome who have a Statement of Special Educational Need

- The Connexions Service is a valuable source of information, advice and support for students up to the age of 19 years

- Students may find it helpful to visit their prospective university or college during the summer vacation to familiarise themselves with the site

- Students are likely to derive more benefit from a gap year if they have made detailed plans about how they will spend their time

- There are some advantages in opting for distance learning courses

- It is recommended that students who have a diagnosis of Asperger syndrome disclose this on their university or college application form

- Interviews may be less problematic if students have sent advance information to the institution about the likely effect of Asperger syndrome on their performance

4

Living Away from Home

If a student chooses to attend a college or university that necessitates a move away from home, accommodation becomes an important consideration. Leaving home is a difficult transition for any young adult, but this is especially the case for students with Asperger syndrome. It is worth contacting the accommodation officer at the college or university as early as possible, and perhaps arranging to visit the various facilities in advance.

Many colleges offer accommodation for the first year and then expect the students to make their own arrangements in subsequent years. However, students with disabilities are given priority consideration if they wish to stay in college accommodation for the duration of their course.

Accommodation

Typical college and university accommodation includes catered halls of residence, self-catering flats, private bed-sits, flats or house-shares. All have their own advantages and disadvantages, and students need to decide which type of accommodation meets their particular needs. Living in a catered hall means that even if money is short or food has not been bought, there will still be the guarantee of getting at least one cooked meal a day. Services and facilities vary according to the type of accommodation chosen. The following should be taken into consideration when making a choice:

- size of hall
- number of students accommodated in hall or flat
- cost
- catering arrangements
- access to self-catering facilities
- distance from the main university site
- privacy: shared facilities such as bedrooms and bathrooms or single rooms and en-suite bathrooms
- separate accommodation for the sexes
- regulations for smoking, overnight visitors, etc.
- communal areas such as common rooms, dining areas and bars
- access to telephones/computers/Internet/television (NB: it is important to remember that all private television sets need their own TV licence)
- laundry facilities
- size of bedroom
- studying facilities
- practising facilities for musical instruments
- level of supervision or warden control

- convenience of public transport
- cost of utility bills.

Halls of residence or private accommodation

Many students with Asperger syndrome benefit from living within a community such as a hall of residence where there are catering and laundry facilities on site. There is the opportunity to interact with other students in communal areas such as the kitchen or common room, but single bedrooms provide privacy and solitude. There will also be residential staff who can, if consent is given, be informed by the Disability Support Staff that students have Asperger syndrome, so that any difficulties they may encounter in the hall of residence can be addressed with understanding.

Students with Asperger syndrome can request that they stay in the same accommodation throughout their course, to avoid having to cope with the upheaval of a move and a change of routine. A balance needs to be found between the opportunity for privacy and solitude and the chance to be with others when company is desired. Although living alone in a bed-sit or flat may seem to be a good option for someone who has difficulty socialising, it is easy to become isolated, withdrawn and lonely. Facing day-to-day practical issues such as shopping, cooking, home organisation and time planning may also be stressful. Finding a suitable hall of residence that meets individual requirements and where it is possible to remain for the duration of the course is often the most satisfactory solution. If students are unhappy with their living arrangements this will inevitably have an effect on their general well-being and their ability to achieve their potential both socially and academically.

Applying for accommodation

Application forms for accommodation can be obtained from individual colleges or universities and these are usually sent out to students after places are firmly accepted in April. Most institutions also have the facility for students to apply for accommodation on-line. It may be necessary to list up to three choices and there will be an opportunity to give a short statement about individual requirements in the relevant section. En-suite facilities are often limited and if this is a priority, disclosure of Asperger syndrome at this stage may be appropriate. It is important to apply as early as possible, and there will be a deadline for the application form to be submitted. Individuals holding a conditional offer of a place at the college or university will usually be sent an accommodation offer as soon as possible following confirmation that entry requirements have been met. It is important to confirm acceptance of the accommodation offer as soon as possible.

Registration

Most colleges and universities require students to provide passport-size photographs before the beginning of the first term. These photographs may be used for the following purposes:

- a library card
- an identity badge, which may be required to gain access to buildings such as the student computer centre or sports centre
- a membership card for the college or university and for the National Union of Students
- an identity card to claim student discounts at certain participating shops or businesses.

Students are often able to register for their course before the beginning of term either by post or on-line. If enrolment has not been possible in advance, provision will be made for this during the first few days of term. Individual colleges and universities will give clear instructions about the registration procedure.

Orientation

Many people with Asperger syndrome have difficulties finding their way around and orientating themselves in a new environment. College and university campuses are often large, daunting, loud, over-stimulating and confusing places. It can be helpful to explore the routes that will need to be taken regularly and to make notes of the best ways to get from place to place. The university or college will probably be able to provide a map locating key places, but if this is too detailed or confusing it might be more useful to make a personalised map, marking out significant landmarks that will be easy to remember and focusing on the main places that will be visited during a typical week. It might also be useful to add the approximate times it takes to complete each trip as this will help with timetabling and punctuality.

The premises of colleges and universities situated in big cities can be spread over a number of miles and can involve a lot of travelling. Campus-based colleges or universities are usually more compact. If a student is aware that they have particular difficulties with certain types of transport, such as the underground or buses, it is advisable to choose an institution where the main buildings are within walking or cycling distance of each other.

Organising belongings

One way to reduce the amount of stress and anxiety associated with managing daily living is to be organised and efficient. Many people with Asperger syndrome find that they have great difficulty with organising their belongings, both at home and at college. When possessions are organised well and kept in designated places there is less risk of misplacing or losing things. (See Box 2.)

Clubs and societies

First-year students usually have the opportunity to enrol at their institution a week before the official beginning of term. This first week is known as Freshers' Week and it provides the opportunity to discover what is on offer in the way of clubs, societies and social life for the next few years. It will also be an important week for exploring the college site, sorting out timetables, adjusting to new living arrangements and, in addition, for meeting many new people.

Students with Asperger syndrome are likely to find this week of new experiences very challenging because of their lack of confidence and their difficulties with social skills. They may feel demoralised and emotionally overwhelmed in the first few days. However, Freshers' Week is a good opportunity for students with Asperger syndrome to explore the provisions available from the disability service and the student counselling service. If a mentoring system has been set up, these sessions may begin in the first week.

Box 2

Guidelines for personal organisation

- Avoid gathering too much unnecessary clutter in personal space; throw things away when they are finished or not needed

- Store items in clearly designated areas, for example clothes that can be hung up in a wardrobe and clothes that can be folded in drawers

- Keep things for college or university separate from leisure interests and use clearly marked storage systems such as bankers boxes, in-trays, folders and files to store work that has been completed

- Use desk tidies to keep small items of stationery in one place on a table or desk

- Keep essential items such as keys, spectacles, wallet and mobile phone in a chosen place where they can be located easily before leaving home

- Pack a bag or rucksack in plenty of time before leaving home; use a personal timetable and diary to ensure that all belongings required for the day are included

- Use personal lockers or pigeon holes for storage at college if these are available

---

Freshers' Fair

Most colleges have a Freshers' Fair where all the college societies and clubs try to recruit new members. These events are run by students through the Students' Union and the exhibitors cover a wide range of interests including debating, religious societies, photography, jazz, choirs, sports, chess and numerous other activities. The Freshers' Fair is usually very crowded and bustling. Students can sometimes feel under pressure to join particular clubs or societies, so it is advisable to have given some thought in advance to which might be of interest. Many students join a large number of clubs and then find that they do not get round to attending any of the meetings. The Students' Union branches of individual institutions publish information about clubs and societies which may be worth looking at before Freshers' Week. It is likely that there will be at least one club that caters for an individual's special interest and this can be a good opportunity to meet other like-minded people.

Students with Asperger syndrome often find it difficult to plan their leisure time and they may have different interests from many of their peers. It is necessary to make time to follow specific interests but it is also important to plan alternative activities that will involve being with others and sharing different experiences.

Food and nutrition

People with Asperger syndrome often have a history of problems with food. These can range from eating a very limited range of foods to a specific eating disorder, such as anorexia nervosa (see Chapter 7, p. 70).

Restricted diets

Some people feel the need to have the same food (and perhaps even the same make of a particular food) at each meal; for example, a specific brand of cereal taken with milk from a particular supermarket for breakfast, and exactly the same filling in a sandwich made from the same type of bread for lunch. While students were still living at home this lack of flexibility might have been relatively easily accommodated, but it is likely to be problematic when they are living away from home and have to fit in with a range of different catering arrangements.

Adjusting to change

The move away from home inevitably requires getting used to different shops, brands and perhaps lack of availability of preferred foods. It is helpful to try to anticipate whether this is likely to become a problem for the student and to try to introduce more variety into the diet in anticipation of the inevitable change in routine.

Avoiding meals

Some students with Asperger syndrome might find they avoid meals altogether if it is too stressful for them to queue up with others to collect their food and eat their meal in a noisy, crowded environment. If this is the case it might be worth discussing these difficulties with the Disability Officer and the catering staff to try and find a way to resolve the problem. For example, it might be possible for students to have a pass to go to the front of the queue, and to have a designated student to accompany them. A quiet area of the room could perhaps be identified where the meal could be taken in relative peace.

Appetite

Some students have little awareness of hunger and will only eat when they are reminded that it is a mealtime and when food is put in front of them. If this is a problem, meals need to be included into the student's daily timetable, with a clear slot allocated to taking snacks, drinks and full meals. The student might need help from a support worker, peer or mentor to plan in advance what needs to be bought and eaten at each meal for the forthcoming week.

Catered accommodation

In catered accommodation meals will usually be served at set times, so it is important to keep a note of mealtimes and not to arrive late. Students with specific dietary requirements should notify the catering staff in their hall of residence and arrange to discuss how their needs can be met.

Managing finances

It is a big change for all students to go from the relative security of living at home to living independently and managing a budget. Budgeting requires organisation, planning and careful management, all of which can be problematic for students with Asperger syndrome.

Bank accounts

Many students will already have a bank account before they go to college or university. Banks and building societies are very keen to recruit new customers and they advertise widely to prospective students, hoping to entice them with tempting offers and free gifts. Students should look carefully at what the banks have to offer, and in particular, whether they are likely to impose heavy penalties if there is any delay in funding the account.

Internet banking

Internet banking offers a convenient and flexible method of keeping a bank account. Money can be paid in at any time, without the restriction of bank opening hours. It also means that the bank balance and information about credits and debits are available whenever there is access to the Internet.

The cost of being a student

University or college life is very expensive; the National Union of Students (NUS) estimates that the average student expenditure for the year 2003/04 was £8,640 for a student living in London and £7,500 for a student living outside London. Students have to learn to live with a bank loan and the knowledge that this needs to be repaid in the future, which can be stressful and anxiety-provoking. Most students are thousands of pounds in debt at the end of their courses. A recent survey showed that, on average, students graduating in London have debts of approximately £15,000 by the time they graduate; £12,000 for those outside London. The interest payable on the student loan rose to 3.1 per cent in the autumn of 2003.

Student loans

The student loan is administered by the Student Loans Company (see Contact Addresses, p. 93). Students living away from home and studying in London are eligible to borrow up to a maximum of £4,930 a year, those studying outside London can borrow up to £4,000. Students who continue to live at home can borrow £3,165.

Supplementary grants

There are additional supplementary grants, such as access and hardship funds or loans, for students with particularly difficult circumstances. These are usually administered by a senior member of staff who has responsibility for student welfare.

Tuition fees

Tuition fees, payable termly in advance, are also a significant expense; the maximum contribution to the tuition fee for 2003/04 is £1,200, although the government is proposing to increase this to £3,000. The amount that has to be paid depends on parental income; currently no contribution is required from parents when their income is less than £20,970.

Most Scottish students have to pay a £2,000 'graduate endowment' after they finish their degrees instead of the upfront fees charged in England and Wales. English students attending universities in Scotland, Wales or Northern Ireland pay a £1,200 upfront fee, usually on a termly basis.

Paying tuition fees

Tuition fees need to be paid by a certain date each term. It is important not to miss the deadline for making this payment. However, it can be very off-putting for people with Asperger syndrome to join a long queue of students waiting to pay in their cheques. This might seem to be such a daunting prospect that the deadline for the payment is missed. If this is a problem it is worth discussing with the Disability Support Staff whether it is possible to get permission to go to the front of the queue, or to arrange a specific time when there will not be a throng of other students waiting.

Some colleges and universities are developing a system of making student loan payments on behalf of the Student Loan Company. This will mean that the first instalment can be paid directly into a nominated bank account instead of by a cheque which needs to be collected. By setting up a direct debit system students can pay both their tuition and accommodation fees directly from their accounts.

Repaying loans

At present, once graduates are in employment and earning over £10,000 a year they have to start repaying their loan according to the students' loan repayment scheme. Repayments are directly related to the graduate's salary and are deducted at source from their income.

Proposed changes to student funding

Significant changes to student funding will come into effect from 2004–5 onwards. The first stage is for the period from 2004–6 and the second is from 2006 onwards. All amounts quoted below are based on 2002–3 rates and are subject to adjustment.

Stage 1: 2004–6:

- A new Higher Education Grant of up to £1,000 will be available to new students from low-income families. There will also be some grant assistance for families with an annual income of up to £20,000 a year.
- From April 2005 graduates earning over £15,000 will have to begin repaying their student loan. This will also apply to all past students who took out loans from 1998 onwards.
- From 2004–5 a step-parent's income will be taken into consideration as part of the means test for grant and maintenance loans.
- The government will continue to fund the £1,200 annual tuition fees for students from families where the annual income is below £20,000, and will make a contribution for those with incomes between £20,000 and £30,000.

Stage 2: From 2006:

England

- Upfront fees will be abolished. Neither parents nor students will have to pay in advance or at any time during the degree course.
- Universities will be able to decide on their own fee levels for different courses; these can range from no charge to £3,000. The government hopes that many universities will charge less than the maximum, particularly for courses which are under-subscribed. In order to set these fees the universities have to meet conditions set out by the Office for Fair Access (OFFA).

- Repayments of fees will be through taxation once the graduate is earning. Payments will be linked to graduates' salaries when they earn £15,000 or more.
- The poorest 30 per cent of full-time students are guaranteed a student loan of a minimum of £3,000 – students from families on incomes between £15,970 and £33,533 will receive a means-tested percentage of the full amount.
- Loans for fees and living expenses are combined so that graduates pay one amount which is calculated, on an interest-free basis, on the money earned and not the money owed.
- A 25-year cap ensures that any debts that are still outstanding 25 years after graduation will be written off.

Wales

- New undergraduates at Welsh universities will no longer pay the upfront fee of £1,200 a year, which will be deferred until they graduate. The Welsh Assembly has pledged not to permit universities to levy higher top-up fees until at least 2007.

Northern Ireland

- There will be no change in the fee system in Northern Ireland, which is not affected by the new legislation. English students entering the two universities in Northern Ireland will continue to pay the existing £1,200 upfront fee.

Scotland

- English students attending Scottish universities in 2006 will continue to pay the £1,200 upfront fee.

Debt

Students with Asperger syndrome often have anxieties about financial matters. It is important to discuss any financial worries with the debt counsellor at college or university, or with the bank account manager. They will be able to give advice about budgeting, debt, hardship grants and hardship loans before a problem escalates. Advice can also be sought from the Student's Union, a financial adviser at the student's bank or through the university or college Disability Support Service.

If it is difficult to meet living expenses out of the student loan and any parental contribution it might be necessary to arrange a personal overdraft. It is important to be aware of the rates of interest that will be incurred on an overdraft and of any penalties that will be imposed if the overdraft limit is exceeded.

Living expenses

Living expenses are the biggest expenditure for students. The NUS estimates that about 80 per cent of a student's income is spent on their accommodation. This percentage increases if the student moves out of a hall of residence into a rented flat or house, where the cost of utility bills will be incurred.

Paying for food, clothes, books, stationery, travel and any socialising is also costly. It can seem as though there is plenty of money in the bank at the beginning of term but it is important to make sure that it does not run out before the end of term.

It is useful to keep detailed accounts of all outgoing expenditure and income using an account book or computer spreadsheet. If it appears that more money is being spent than is coming in, it will be necessary to make adjustments early to prevent the problem escalating.

A simple chart can be used to keep track of weekly outgoings:

	Food/ Drink	Rent	Travel	Books/ Stationery	Clothes	Extras	Total
Week 1							
Week 2							
Week 3							
Week 4							
Total							

Student discounts

Student discounts are often available in shops, restaurants, cinemas and theatres. Many local businesses are aware that they need to attract students and they may have special offers for them. It is a good idea to borrow books from the library, and if they do need to be bought they may be available at second-hand bookshops.

Student employment

It might be worth considering getting a part-time job to supplement the student loan. Colleges and universities often have job shops that will try to find suitable work for their students. Working for the college or university through the Students' Union is another option. Although a job will ease any financial worries it will impinge on the time available for study. If the job leads to a problem with time management or causes increased stress it is not advisable to pursue this route. However, working for a few hours in an environment where there is contact with other students or the public can be an opportunity to engage in interaction that has a clear purpose and structure. This can be a good opportunity to practise skills such as eye contact and brief conversations.

If employment in term time is not practical it is still possible to work during the vacations. As it can be difficult to deal with the lack of structure and routine when there are no lectures or tutorials to attend, finding suitable employment can be a positive way of occupying time, while easing the financial burdens for the following term.

Clothes

Clothes can present a number of problems for people with Asperger syndrome:

- *Fabric sensitivity* – if individuals are particularly sensitive to textures and materials they may only be comfortable wearing certain fabrics.
- *Lack of flexibility* – many people become restricted in the range of clothes that are worn; for example, wearing only one style of trousers and T-shirt day after day, regardless of the social situation or weather conditions. The thought of wearing clothes that look, smell or feel different can induce extreme anxiety and panic.
- *Self-imposed standards* – some students have a constant need to change their clothes, either resulting from a fear that they are stained or dirty or simply in an endeavour to find an outfit that meets all their sensory demands. This can result in a number of different outfits being worn in one day.

> 'On my first day, I wore clothes that were perceived to be "trendy" by societal tribal instinct and I generally wasn't being myself at all.'
> *EM*

- *Fashion* – a lack of awareness of fashion, or interest in blending in with the types of clothes worn by fellow students, can result in unusual choices of clothes that seem either odd or simply idiosyncratic. The designer and logo culture of clothes usually has very little lure for people with Asperger syndrome.
- *Fit* – poorly fitting clothes, either very tight fitting or loose, may be worn when there is hypersensitivity to texture or to the feeling of clothes against the skin.

Listening to the advice of siblings and other students and observing the current 'uniform' worn by the majority of students can help the student with Asperger syndrome tune in to the types of clothes that will make them less conspicuous. This can be a simple first step towards integration. However, there is no need to feel pressurised to be the same as everyone else; everyone is entitled to choose their own style of clothing, which is merely a means of self-expression and individuality.

Personal hygiene

It is not unusual for students with Asperger syndrome to have significant problems with personal hygiene when they start living away from home. At home they may have had an unchanging routine where there were prescribed times for bathing, showering, hair washing and cleaning teeth. Without this structure and routine, personal hygiene can be neglected. Students may have some of the following difficulties:

- knowing or remembering when it is appropriate to wash, especially after exercise and in hot weather
- having an aversion to the feel or temperature of water or the smell of soap, shampoo or toothpaste
- being reluctant to wash private parts if this feels inappropriate or uncomfortable
- having an extreme need for privacy with a reluctance to share bathroom facilities
- being reluctant to change clothes that are comfortable and feel and smell familiar
- feeling the need to wash or change clothes constantly, in response to minimal soiling or stains
- lack of attention to dental hygiene, especially if there is hypersensitivity in the mouth that makes brushing uncomfortable or even painful

- having an aversion to nail and hair cutting, particularly when there has been a childhood history of fear of being touched or a fear of the feel or sound of scissors.

The best management for these problems is to devise a clearly structured routine that covers showering or bathing, washing hair, changing clothes and cleaning teeth. The routine needs to be followed regardless of whether the student feels there is a need to do any of these things. It is safer to err on the side of being too fastidious than to abandon daily hygiene. A routine that has been timetabled to fit into the student's day will be of equal value to those students who do not wash enough as to those that wash too often. If there are sensory problems related to scents or perfumes it is possible to purchase fragrance-free toiletries.

Health and fitness

Registering with a doctor

One of the first things that a student needs to do when he or she moves away from home is to register with a doctor. If students become ill it is important for the doctor to have immediate access to their medical history, particularly if regular medication is prescribed. Most colleges and universities have a medical service and the students' handbook will give the appropriate information and contact details. University medical practices or health centres often run health-related courses covering issues that are relevant to students' lives, such as smoking, alcohol, diet and relaxation. These services will only be available to those students who register.

Medical certificates

Some universities may require medical certificates if there have been any prolonged absences (often over seven days) due to illness, particularly if this has affected the completion of coursework or performance in examinations.

Dentists

It may also be necessary to arrange to see a dentist, although many students manage by having their dental appointments with their family dentist in the vacations. The college or university will have names and contact details of recommended dentists who see NHS patients.

Exercise

Regular exercise is important for health and fitness. There are usually excellent sporting facilities at colleges and universities, such as playing fields, various hard courts and fitness suites. Some have their own swimming pools. Although team sports do not appeal to most people with Asperger syndrome there should be the opportunity to find some form of exercise that will both maintain levels of fitness and provide a regular leisure activity with the opportunity to meet people. Sports that focus on individual performance such as golf, martial arts, cycling, swimming, yoga and running can be very rewarding and are a good way of reducing tension and stress levels.

Key points from Chapter 4

- Moving into a hall of residence is often a good step towards independent living

- Students with Asperger syndrome may be offered the opportunity to remain in a hall of residence throughout their course

- Freshers' Week is a good opportunity to make contact with Disability Support Staff and to join clubs that relate to special interests

- Students need to make sure that they eat regularly – fully catered accommodation may make this easier

- It is a good idea to make a daily or weekly timetable and include personal hygiene so that a routine is established

- Managing a budget and taking responsibility for finances is easier if students are well informed about likely expenditure and sources of income before they start their course

5

Academic Issues

New university and college students are usually assigned a personal tutor whose role is partly pastoral and partly academic. The more tutors understand about Asperger syndrome and its effects on individual students, the more they will be able to support their tutees. The information leaflet in the Resources section of this book (p. 77) is designed to provide basic information for tutors, and the more personal information leaflet, which can be completed with the Disability Coordinator or other support staff, will give tutors an insight into the particular ways in which tutees are affected by Asperger syndrome. If recommendations have been made following an Assessment of Need, these will have to be discussed with the personal tutor, who will liaise with other academic staff as appropriate to make sure that, as far as possible, the recommended support is put in place. This might include sitting in an aisle seat in lectures and examinations, use of technical aids, recording of lectures and permission to work alone instead of in a group.

The role of the personal tutor

The precise role of the personal tutor varies from one institution to another. Generally tutors arrange to see their tutees at least once a term to talk through any problems they have relating to their studies or life at university. Sometimes the tutor is also one of the student's teachers but this may not always be the case, so discussion about work will tend to be more general than specific. Tutors who have a tutee with Asperger syndrome are likely to find that they need to devote more than the average amount of time to supporting the student. It may therefore be appropriate for these tutors to have fewer than the normal number of students assigned to them. Initially a short weekly discussion may be helpful, but gradually, if other support has been put in place, students may find they need to see their tutor less frequently.

Students normally keep the same personal tutor throughout their course, unless the tutor leaves or takes up a different appointment within the institution, or unless a change is considered necessary for personal reasons. Tutors' systems for making appointments should be made clear to students. They may set aside a period each week when they are available to see students on a 'drop-in' basis. Alternatively, they may have an appointment system. They may prefer students to contact them by email rather than by telephone.

Routine and time management

Routine and predictability are very important for people with Asperger syndrome. The photo-copiable weekly timetable in the Resource section of the book (p. 77) is designed to cover every hour in the day from seven o'clock in the morning until midnight. Students may find it helpful to make copies of this for each week of term so that an overall plan for each week can be made.

Box 3

Estimating how long activities are likely to take can be a problem for people with Asperger syndrome. Here is a useful exercise to see whether you have developed this skill:

1. Make a list of every single thing you normally do in the course of a week – eating, sleeping, shopping, lectures, reading, travelling, etc.
2. Estimate how long you spend each week doing these things and add the time, in hours, to the list.
3. Add up the hours.

There are 168 hours in a week, so anything wildly different, whether more or less, is an indication that your estimation of time is not very accurate. If this is the case the weekly timetable is likely to be helpful, but it may take a few weeks before it accurately records what you will be able to do in the given time.

Generally lectures and other university or college commitments remain the same for each week, but some institutions operate a two-week timetable. The blank timetable provided is particularly useful if there are frequent changes to the weekly routine.

Inevitably last-minute changes to timetables, lecture rooms or teaching staff will sometimes occur. It is important for students with Asperger syndrome to know how they can expect to be informed of such changes. For example, should they check their email or is a notice put up on a notice board? Coping with the unexpected can be difficult, but knowing how changes are likely to be communicated can be reassuring.

Field trips, reading weeks, exam times and the vacations are all times when the usual term-time routine is disrupted. Advance information and preparation about the arrangements for these events will help the student to prepare for these changes. Field trips can be particularly challenging as they involve new locations and living arrangements. It is helpful for the trip leader to be aware of any anxieties in advance and to monitor the student carefully throughout the trip.

> '**I sometimes feel that having Asperger syndrome is an advantage when it comes to studying. I do not have to fit my study in around a hectic social life and when I am working on a project that interests me I will work at it to the exclusion of everything else.**' *CH*

Organisation of private study

Studying at college and university can seem frighteningly unsupervised. Deadlines for handing in written work may be set weeks or months in advance, and nobody checks to see whether you have made a start on a piece of coursework or monitors how it is coming along. This can be a daunting prospect for all first-year students, but as time management is often a particular problem for students with Asperger syndrome, the lack of imposed structure at university needs to be replaced by positive strategies for self management. Students will need to consider the following.

Time

What is the best time of day for private study? Some people work best at night when there are fewer distractions; others like to get up early. It is best to try to take a day off studying each week to relax and do other things. Depending on lecture commitments, which vary widely across courses, it will probably be necessary to spend about 20 hours a week studying. The weekly timetable can be used to allocate 'slots' for studying, as for all other activities that need to be planned.

> 'One of my biggest problems was with organisation. I had difficulty meeting deadlines for essays and assignments and I soon fell very far behind. Eventually I was given some help with planning a detailed work timetable which I stuck to very rigidly and this helped me to complete work on time' *JA*

Place

Students with Asperger syndrome may find it easier to work in their own study-bedroom than in more public places such as the library, but it may take time to decide which is the best option. Some institutions have dedicated computer cluster rooms for students with disabilities, and these can provide a quiet, safe and supportive working environment.

Objectives

However long or short a private study period is to be, it is important to set goals. For example, 'by the end of the week I will have made a draft essay plan, taken the relevant books out of the library, read a certain number of articles and taken notes on them'. Short-term objectives for a study session might be to read an article, take notes and plan how the information will be used in an essay.

Materials

Students who work best in their own room will normally have all the equipment they need available during study periods. Those who prefer to study in the library or elsewhere on the college site may need a checklist of study materials they need to take with them, for example, highlighters, sheets of A3 paper for mind-maps, pencils, calculator, photocopied articles etc.

Sound

Some students can concentrate best while listening to music, whereas others find this distracting and like to work in silence. For students with Asperger syndrome ostensibly quiet places such as libraries may have a lot of background noise that other people do not seem to notice: whispering voices, the hum of computers, the buzzing of lighting and the clicking of entry and exit turnstiles. Earplugs can be a useful way of minimising the annoyance and distraction of these unwanted sounds.

Breaks

Learning is more effective if short breaks are taken regularly, say every 45 minutes. As students with Asperger syndrome may become totally absorbed in their work, perhaps even forgetting what they had originally planned to do, it may be helpful to set the alarm on their mobile phone to remind them to take a break and to refocus on their objectives for the study session. Obviously this would not be an appropriate strategy for use in a library.

Filing

It is important to develop a system for storing and filing notes, references and essays so that these are available when needed. This aspect of organisation is as likely to be computer-based as paper-based.

Study skills

Students with Asperger syndrome do not all experience the same difficulties in relation to their studies. Learning styles and preferences vary widely, as do other cognitive strengths and needs. However, some problems seem to be reported regularly by students with Asperger syndrome and these are outlined below, with some suggested strategies for addressing some of them.

Attention

Students with Asperger syndrome do not generally have a poor attention span, but they have their *own* attention span.

Absorption in an activity or subject of interest can lead students to reach phenomenal academic heights in a particular subject, but they are likely to have difficulty spreading their attention across all aspects of their course.

> 'Nobody believed I could have problems paying attention, given the complete absorption with which I could focus on some things. But I could not shift my attention from one subject to another by an act of will.'
> *Clare Sainsbury*

Relevance and purpose

Students with Asperger syndrome are unlikely to work effectively if they cannot see the relevance of what they are expected to learn. A syllabus drawn up by others is likely to contain certain areas of study that are not of particular interest to some students, yet they may be compulsory components of the degree course. Tutors should be able to give a clear rationale for the inclusion of certain modules or units of study, showing how these relate, however apparently obliquely, to the 'bigger picture' of the degree subject as a whole.

Audience

One of the core features of Asperger syndrome is a lack of awareness that people have different knowledge and experiences from oneself. If a student is very knowledgeable about a subject, he or she may not see any point in trying to demonstrate this knowledge to a tutor, whether orally or in writing, yet this is the primary purpose of coursework assignments and examinations.

Furthermore, the 'audience' for whom the student is writing should not actually be the recipient (the assessor). Students need to be taught that their 'pretend' audience is a hypothetical reader who has sufficient lay knowledge to make sense of the coursework, but who is not (unlike the person who will be marking it) an expert. With this hypothetical reader in mind, students should give sufficient information to demonstrate their knowledge clearly; they will not omit to clarify certain points as a result of assuming that 'the marker knows it anyway'.

This is bound to be a difficult concept for students with Asperger syndrome to grasp, and the concept of 'audience' may need to be included in any study skills tuition given.

Memory

Some students with Asperger syndrome have excellent visual memory skills and benefit in their learning from the use of visual aids such as colour, highlighters, drawings, diagrams and graphs where appropriate. Techniques such as mind-mapping are often very effective.

Mind-mapping, or concept mapping, was developed by Tony Buzan in the 1960s and since that time has become a popular study technique (Buzan 1974). Mind-mapping uses an individual's visual–spatial skills to help them create a pictorial representation of ideas and thoughts. The basic principle of mind-mapping involves writing a word or phrase as a central idea in the middle of a page and then generating further new and related ideas branching off from the centre, using lines, colours, capital letters, symbols and arrows to make the appropriate connections. This highly visual and immediate method of representing information often suits the learning style of people with Asperger syndrome. Personalising information in a way that reflects an individual's thought processes can help with planning, organising, note-taking, essay-planning and memorising.

Some students who have a weak auditory working memory find it helpful to record key parts of lectures or tutorials on mini-disk. They can then replay their recordings at home, making mind-maps or notes to help them remember the content. It is not recommended to record whole lectures because it is bound to be difficult to find the time to listen to them.

> 'Before my final exams I covered all the walls in my room with giant sheets of paper covered in complex diagrams of the philosophical arguments I was studying. It freaked everyone out who came into my room during that term, but I had finally learnt not to care.'
> *Clare Sainsbury*

Generalising

It is usually difficult for students with Asperger syndrome to arrive at general principles through specific information. Information tends to be accumulated on a 'piecemeal' basis and conceptual links may not be made. The result of this lack of cohesive thought is that students may not be able to apply their knowledge in new and subtly different situations. For example, a student may not recognise the departmental receptionist in the supermarket because recognition is restricted to the precise environment of previous encounters (i.e. at the reception desk). This lack of cohesive thought has significant implications for academic learning and is likely to need to be addressed in study skills tuition sessions.

Inference

Students with Asperger syndrome have difficulty understanding figurative language and 'reading between the lines'. They are inclined to interpret language literally and have problems with inference-based comprehension. For example, authors of journal articles may make a positive comment about one aspect of another author's work, but may imply criticism by what is *not* said. Students may need to be taught explicitly what to look out for when reading academic texts so that they do not simply accept the written word at face value.

Prioritising

Because of their tendency to focus exclusively on a subject of interest, students with Asperger syndrome are likely to find it difficult to accept that their teachers may expect them to prioritise differently. It is important for tutors to give clear guidelines about what students are expected to cover in their studies. Some readings may be essential, while others may be less important; some tasks may be set as a useful exercise to practise skills and others will be compulsory pieces of coursework.

Structuring writing

A well-structured piece of writing will outline the scope of the assignment in the introduction, and there will be a coherent progression of ideas culminating in a conclusion which draws them together. The various sections of the work need to be well balanced, as does any argument or discussion. Students with Asperger syndrome may find that they lose overall coherence and cohesion in their writing through becoming too absorbed in detail. The best way to avoid this is to spend time planning the piece as a whole unit before starting to write. Planning written assignments is generally a much more effective use of time than proof-reading them after they are written.

Examinations

Examinations demand a range of skills, many of which are difficult for students with Asperger syndrome to acquire without help. Time management is critical. It is important to spend the appropriate amount of time on each part of the paper, taking into account the weighting of marks. A choice usually needs to be made as to which questions to answer. Answers should be planned so that they are balanced and so that they contain all the required information.

Examination questions will contain key words relating to content (for example, *Dutch genre painting, the eco-system of the Amazon rainforest* or *the incidence of tuberculosis in nineteenth-century Britain*). Another set of key words, which is just as important, but may seem less obvious, relates to 'instruction'. In other words, how is the content to be presented? Instruction words include *discuss, analyse, justify, describe, report, account for* and *explain.* When reading the questions the key content words and instruction words need to be noticed and understood. It may be a good idea to highlight them in different colours.

Throughout the examination, timing should be monitored. A first-class answer to one question will not compensate for the omission of other answers because of lack of time.

Handwriting

It is very common for students with Asperger syndrome to have problems with handwriting. It will often be appropriate for them to use a laptop computer in lectures and examinations.

The Disabled Students' Allowance will often include funding for individual tuition. Specialist tutors need to have a detailed knowledge of Asperger syndrome and its likely effect on study skills. Most tutors have specialised in teaching students with dyslexia, whose learning style and cognitive profile is likely to be quite different. Tuition for students with Asperger syndrome is likely to focus on the areas of study outlined above.

Tuition should always focus on the development of strategies rather than on providing support in the completion of individual pieces of coursework, as the objective is for the student to become a more independent learner.

Working in groups

Working in a group with other students can be very challenging for students with Asperger syndrome. In particular, problems with interacting with others can make small-group work difficult. They might be inhibited about speaking in front of others and, as a result, withdraw from group participation and discussion. Alternatively, they may have a dominating style where they talk excessively and the other members of the group do not have the opportunity to contribute. There may also be problems related to motivation, where students with Asperger syndrome only engage with the group for the activities which they find particularly interesting, but opt out when they lose interest in the topic under discussion. They can also find it difficult to know when it is appropriate to ask a question or to make a contribution to the discussion.

Group leaders or tutors and their tutees need to set ground rules for the organisation and running of group work sessions, with particular attention being paid to students who find this style of working difficult. The following issues could be addressed by the whole group to encourage consensus and co-operation:

- punctuality
- preparation
- aims
- participation
- identification of roles for all group members
- validity of opinions and views
- confidentiality
- clarification if something is not understood
- strategies for problem-solving and management of disagreements or misunderstandings.

See also 'Tutorials' below.

Libraries

For students who do not feel comfortable working in libraries, the institution's Disability Support Service can often arrange for extended borrowing times, extended library hours or reference book loans.

Lectures

Lecture theatres or rooms are often designed to teach a large number of students at one time. There can be problems with concentration, particularly if the subject matter is not of specific interest to the student. There are also issues regarding attention, absorption of information and distractibility. Sensory sensitivity can cause distractibility during a lecture, particularly if the student's attention is diverted by irritating sounds such as creaking chairs or talking, or smells such as smoke or perfumes.

At times of stress it can be helpful for students to have an open exit policy, where they can leave the lecture theatre and return when they have recovered. It is important that the student has a

'I had great difficulty in absorbing all the information without having any visual prompts. I was very distracted by the proximity of so many other students and got irritated when they talked amongst themselves and didn't pay attention to the lecturer. This was made easier when I had an aisle seat but I still found it very difficult to take in so much verbal information.' *CH*

safe place to go to, either within the room or outside; these areas should be designated as places of refuge where the student can relax and be undisturbed.

It is often helpful if the student can have copies of any overheads or handouts before a lecture begins.

On a more positive note, the content of lectures is usually much more structured than lessons at school; interaction and contributions from the students is not expected even though students often ask questions, and the increasing use of effective audio-visual aids such as Microsoft PowerPoint facilitates learning through visual channels.

> 'Note-taking in lectures was a nightmare, I couldn't write fast enough and afterwards I found that I couldn't read what I had written. This problem was solved when I was able to record the lectures with a mini-disk and play them back later.' *EM*

Tutorials

The tutorial system of teaching often suits the learning styles of people with Asperger syndrome, as a ratio of five to ten students to a tutor can be a very effective way to learn. There may also be an opportunity to talk to the tutor immediately after the tutorial to check that everything has been understood and to get some constructive feedback.

However, the anonymity afforded to students in large lecture theatres is lacking in a tutorial setting. Students are all expected to contribute to the discussion and to share their knowledge. They are likely to have to work with their peers in preparation for tutorials, and may even be asked to chair the session themselves. Tutorials can therefore be extremely stressful for students with Asperger syndrome and it is important that potential problems are addressed with the tutor before the sessions begin, and, as in planning group projects, ground rules for conducting the sessions need to be established.

> 'Explaining my diagnosis to the others in my tutorial group helped them to understand me. They saw that there was a reason why I seemed awkward with them and they became more supportive.' *JA*

Feedback

The purpose of feedback is to:

- enable students to monitor their progress and developing skills
- identify strengths and weaknesses without undermining confidence
- explain exactly what needs to be worked on to make changes
- guide the student to improve and develop his or her work.

Students with Asperger syndrome often have difficulty interpreting written feedback on coursework if this is not very explicit. As a general principle, feedback should highlight the aspects of the task that the student has carried out well and that do not need to be improved upon. If all feedback is negative, the student may not realise that he or she has met any of the assessment criteria, and may find the grade awarded confusing. It is helpful to students if they can be told to what extent an omission or error has affected their grade. Feedback should be constructive, showing how the student could meet more of the assessment criteria in the next piece of coursework. Students should also be aware of the assessment criteria before they start to plan and write their assignment.

Non-specific feedback includes phrases such as:

- 'Your essay lacks coherence.'
- 'Have you proof-read this?'
- 'This essay is not well balanced.'

A student receiving this feedback will be unlikely to have any idea what to do to avoid receiving it again.

Specific, constructive feedback is shown in the following:

> You show in this essay that you have very detailed knowledge about . . . but you were asked to discuss both . . . and . . . As you have not covered the second part of the question your mark has been reduced by half. To make sure this does not happen again, you will need to read the question in detail and plan your essay to cover everything that is asked for.

Here, there is a positive comment followed by feedback which directs the student to the likely cause of the problem. Feedback like this is constructive rather than negative.

Students may also be required to give feedback to their peers in tutorials. As students with Asperger syndrome have difficulty gauging how their comments are likely to be received by others, it is essential that clear ground rules for giving and receiving feedback are established at the outset by the supervising tutor.

Examination arrangements

Exams are stressful for all students, but one of the most challenging aspects of taking exams for students with Asperger syndrome is the total change in routine. For a few weeks there will be a completely new timetable to accommodate revision time and exam-taking. Students may become extremely anxious at this time and are likely to need more support.

Students with Asperger syndrome will need time to study the exam timetable, to visit the exam location and to find out where they will be sitting. They should be notified of any room changes as soon as possible, preferably individually and in writing.

Students may benefit from the opportunity to complete a practice paper using the official booklets used in the examinations. They can then familiarise themselves with, for example, using treasury tags to attach additional booklets.

Special requirements for oral exams also need to be identified. The examiner needs prior knowledge of the student's Asperger syndrome and information about how the condition may affect the student's performance, particularly with regard to:

- unusual eye contact
- body language
- speech or style of presentation
- tendency to dominate the conversation or interrupt
- reverting to a topic of special interest
- difficulty understanding subtle questions; explicit and unambiguous language should be used
- misinterpretation of humour or light-hearted comments

Box 4

Special arrangements for taking examinations

- early arrival time at the examination venue

- being accompanied to the exam by a friend or support worker

- being given individual instructions by the invigilator to make sure the exam process has been fully understood

- permission to leave the examination room accompanied by an invigilator if required

- provision of a separate exam room if the student is likely to distract the other examinees (perhaps needing to move around, using a computer, a timer or speaking) or if the student might be distracted in the main exam room

- the opportunity to have an aisle seat or a seat near the door

- use of a timer as a prompt for when it is time to move on to a new section or question

- extra time, which would be appropriate if the student has difficulty organising time, works very slowly, has a slow handwriting speed or finds the time restriction particularly anxiety-provoking

- use of ear plugs to reduce noise distractions

- a note attached to scripts to inform the markers that the student has Asperger syndrome so that the likely effects can be taken into account

---

Arrangements need to be discussed with the Disability Support Staff, who will make appropriate recommendations to the department responsible for administering the examinations.

Plagiarism

Plagiarism has become a serious problem that needs to be addressed by schools, colleges and universities, particularly with such easy access to other people's work through the World Wide Web. Plagiarism is the use of other people's ideas, writing and inventions without giving a clear reference to the original work. Written assignments that are found to include plagiarised content can result in a student's suspension or expulsion from courses.

In any piece of coursework other people's ideas and theories are likely to be discussed, so to avoid plagiarising it is vitally important that the source of the work is always acknowledged. Reference should be made to the original information source whenever any of the following are used in a student's written work:

- any mention of another person's ideas, theories, opinions or writings
- any diagrams, charts, statistics or drawings compiled by other people
- any direct quotations, either spoken or written
- any paraphrasing that amounts to small changes of vocabulary or word order, and where the original work is still clearly recognisable.

When another author's work is used verbatim, quotation marks should be used. However, information which has come to be accepted as public or general knowledge does not need to be referenced.

Students with Asperger syndrome may find that they have plagiarised inadvertently. They may find it difficult to rephrase ideas in their own words, particularly if they have a published text open in front of them. They may also find it difficult to see why, if an idea has already been eloquently phrased, they should not use the same wording in their own work. To avoid the temptation of using whole chunks of other authors' work it is better to write using only notes, having closed the textbook or journal.

Key points from Chapter 5

- Personal tutors play an important part in supporting students with Asperger syndrome

- The management of time in essay writing, examinations and daily and weekly routines is likely to need to be addressed in a practical and explicit way

- Students need to find a routine for private study that suits their learning style, which may at first involve some trial and error

- Students with Asperger syndrome are likely to benefit from specialist study skills tuition focused on extracting information from texts, structuring written assignments and examination techniques

- Working in small groups is likely to be challenging, so potential problems should be discussed with tutors

- Special examination arrangements, such as a private room or an aisle seat, may be appropriate for some students

6

Social Issues

Emotional vulnerability

Expressing emotions

It is very important to stress that although people with Asperger syndrome often have difficulty expressing emotions they are not in any way unfeeling or thick-skinned. At times they can seem to be unemotional and yet at other times they appear to overreact to apparently trivial situations. They may appear to be cold or insensitive: for example, they might have difficulty expressing sadness or shock when they hear bad news; their emotional profile is undoubtedly different from that of other people but it does not follow that they are devoid of emotion or feelings, which is a common misconception about people with Asperger syndrome. On the contrary, many people with Asperger syndrome have very powerful emotions; they just display their feelings in different ways.

Hypersensitivity to sensory stimuli can cause people with Asperger syndrome to lose their temper or to be irritated by things that would be missed or ignored by others. For example, noises, odours or the proximity of other people can cause anger and frustration resulting in outbursts of temper or withdrawal. This is discussed in greater detail in Chapter 1.

Talking to others about Asperger syndrome

> One way in which more able individuals with autism are able to help themselves is to be explicit with other people about the nature of their difficulties. (Howlin 1997)

To tell or not to tell

When students start a university or college course they face the dilemma of whether or not to disclose their disability. They may feel that this is an opportunity to start afresh – to try to begin life as a student without acknowledging to anyone that they have Asperger syndrome. This is an understandable point of view. However, students with Asperger syndrome are increasingly being offered appropriate support so that they are now more likely than previously to complete their degree courses successfully; many will have applied for the DSA and their tutors and lecturers will be aware of their diagnosis.

> 'People with Asperger syndrome know what the problems are but we cannot expect other people to understand unless we explain it to them.' *EM*

The subject of disclosure raises a number of questions:

- Is it right to disclose?
- When is the best time to disclose?
- Who should make the disclosure – the student, their mentor, parent, the disability officer, the counsellor?

- Should the disclosure be spoken or written?
- To whom should the disclosure be made?
- Should a number of people be told?
- What exactly should be said?
- What will disclosure achieve?
- Will confidentiality be maintained?
- Will I be judged or labelled?

> 'My tutors were generally sympathetic and interested when I told them about my diagnosis, and I was able to get permission on medical grounds to have an aisle seat in all my exams.' *Clare Sainsbury*

Others' preconceived ideas

People often have preconceived ideas and prejudices about the features and symptoms of an autism spectrum disorder, mainly as a result of extensive coverage in films, newspaper articles and television programmes. People may make certain assumptions about the condition and may fail to accept a person with Asperger syndrome as an individual. It can often be more difficult explaining about Asperger syndrome to people who think they know what the condition is than to those with no prior knowledge.

Before arriving at college or university the student's diagnosis may have been disclosed to peers, teachers, relatives, friends of the family and perhaps acquaintances, but the disclosure will usually have been communicated by a parent or guardian. Perhaps for the first time the student is now responsible for handling disclosure alone. Students who have found it difficult to explain their difficulties in the past may be tempted not to tell others of their diagnosis, and try instead to start their new life with a 'clean slate'.

It might be useful to go through the list of questions above with a trusted adult, perhaps a parent, relative, friend or support worker, in an attempt to understand all the pros and cons of disclosure before making any rash decisions. The reality is that it will be appropriate to disclose different amounts and types of information depending upon whether it is to a casual acquaintance (where any disclosure would probably be unnecessary) or to a fellow student or member of staff.

> 'I have realised I cannot function easily without support at university. I am trying to get help for my second year and hope that some mentoring might help my situation.' *EM*

Accessing support

Perhaps the best argument in favour of disclosure when applying to college or university is that the student will be able to access the full range of support that is now available for all those with a recognised disability. Although keeping quiet might seem to be a good idea initially, the reality is that the condition does not go away simply because it is not mentioned, and it will be more difficult to access support when it is needed if no one has been aware of the diagnosis.

Application forms for colleges and universities have a section where information can be given about any special facilities or support the student is likely to need. This might include extra equipment, support with aspects of study or counselling services. It is also recommended that students contact the Disability Officer at their chosen colleges or universities to discuss their needs before completing the application process (see Chapter 2). All information given either on the application form or directly to the Disability Co-ordinator will be confidential.

If information is given to the college or university before the student's course begins it can be filtered through to the academic and support staff before the beginning of the first term. The appropriate support, involving the Disability Officer and any mentoring or counselling service, can be put place in from the outset. With this support network behind the student the whole process of disclosure can be addressed. (For more information on accessing support, student counselling and mentoring see Chapter 2.)

Friendships and relationships

Forming and maintaining friendships

Difficulties forming and maintaining friendships and relationships are often the most overwhelming aspect of Asperger syndrome. These problems are often less acute while individuals are living at home, where their social contacts revolve around family friends and relatives.

> 'Socially, I floundered, and continued to get seriously depressed (as I had done since my teens) by my failure to do what "normal" people did (and by my guilty secret – that I didn't always want to do what normal people did).' *Clare Sainsbury*

Living away from familiar people and routines for the first time and trying to develop a new social network can be one of the most challenging aspects of attending college or university. The isolation of the student with Asperger syndrome may be magnified by the fact that other students appear to find it easy to make friends and are apparently able to establish new social lives effortlessly. Maintaining close friendships requires highly sophisticated social skills and levels of empathy that can be daunting and confusing to the individual with Asperger syndrome.

> 'Looking back now, it has only taken six months for me to reach the first parapet of the social tower, and the next corkscrew staircase beckons, to carry me to new heights. I am now confident, yet not complacent.' *EM*

Desire to make friends

People with Asperger syndrome usually have a strong desire to make friendships, but their difficulties with social interaction can make this difficult.

Many adults with Asperger syndrome do form friendships and intimate relationships. Their relationships are more likely to succeed if there is mutual understanding of how the syndrome affects both parties, and when strategies have been developed to minimise misunderstandings. Sustaining close friendships can be difficult if the affected partner does not understand or is insensitive to their partner's emotional state. Subtle non-verbal communication indicating irritation, boredom, annoyance, pleasure or sadness may be completely missed by people with Asperger syndrome, giving the impression that they are insensitive and uncaring, when they have simply been unable to read the other person's mind.

> 'I felt that half of me wanted to socialise but that the other half wanted me to withdraw.' *EM*

From the perspective of someone with Asperger syndrome, the following points are worth considering.

Don't expect too much too quickly

Difficulty understanding how friendships and relationships develop can lead to unrealistic expectations. For example, interpreting a very casual encounter as more significant than it

> **'I cannot socialise at all on an intimate level, or at any level above introductions.'** *EM*

really is, and consequently feeling let down and disappointed when the other person attaches little significance to the social exchange.

Don't jump to conclusions

People with Asperger syndrome occasionally make very quick decisions about whether they like or dislike someone based on first impressions. It is important to take enough time to get to know people slowly and to avoid making rash assumptions about people.

Try to make eye contact

It can be helpful to concentrate on making eye contact, as this is the most effective way of interpreting how the other person is feeling and responding.

> **'I don't like to look at people when they talk to me because I don't listen with my eyes.'** *TH*

Consider attending social groups for people with Asperger syndrome

Asperger syndrome support groups are recognised as being extremely helpful and supportive. These groups may be supported by a professional who either leads or sits in on the sessions. Others do not have any professionals involved. Occasionally meetings will be set up initially with a professional in attendance, who gradually withdraws from the group once it is fully established. The meetings might take place in a pub, restaurant or café or be arranged around a specific activity or excursion.

Acknowledge that it's OK to spend some time on your own

Many people with Asperger syndrome need time on their own and enjoy solitary activities, and it is important to acknowledge that this is perfectly acceptable. It is simply not their style to be gregarious and feel the need to be in the company of others all the time.

> **'I was most happy avoiding my peers, investigating the wonderful libraries and bookshops and going for long solitary walks around and around the college gardens.'** *Clare Sainsbury*

Not all friendships need to be intimate

It is important to use the experience of college to make casual acquaintances and friendships, and to treat these interactions as learning experiences.

Make friends through doing things together

Joining special interest groups or clubs can be a good way of meeting people with similar interests.

Engage the help of a sensitive peer

Peer support from a fellow student or mentor can be a good way of learning about social skills, and strategies can be planned together to make future encounters more successful.

Think about structured training in social skills

Attending social skills training groups, and in particular learning about how other people think and perceive things, can be helpful. However, group therapy sessions with people who do not have an autistic spectrum disorder are often not successful (Gillberg 2002).

If people are given a chance to understand, they probably will

Providing information and education to staff and fellow students about Asperger syndrome can make people much more tolerant and understanding of the difficulties encountered by those with the condition.

Learn more about yourself

Learning about how Asperger syndrome affects individuals in different ways through reading or through mentoring or counselling sessions can be a useful way of developing compensatory strategies.

The World Wide Web has its uses

Internet chat-rooms can provide a forum for communicating with others who have either interests or hobbies in common or who also have Asperger syndrome. This can be very supportive, reducing feelings of isolation and loneliness without the pressure of face-to-face contact.

> 'I used to spend hours and hours online – I suddenly had lots of friends from all over the world who wanted to hear from me. This was a new experience and I became much more confident through my computer than I could be in real life.' *EC*

> 'My mindset is split between *wanting* to socialise and *having* to socialise. I want to be able to socialise, but I have a mental block, my defences are almost too sensitive and I give up.' *EM*

From the perspective of friends of someone with Asperger syndrome, the following points are worth considering;

He's not being rude; he's just being honest

Being tactful, diplomatic and avoiding upsetting people are important in social interactions, but people with Asperger syndrome have great difficulty with this subtle aspect of communication. It is important for friends and acquaintances of people with Asperger syndrome to understand that blunt or insensitive remarks reflect honesty as opposed to rudeness or unkindness. The tactful white lie is a device that is rarely used by people with this condition.

Be open about your concerns

Both parties in a friendship need to be clear and explicit in their use of language, feelings and expectations. If too many assumptions are made about how the other person is feeling, this can lead to misunderstanding or even a complete breakdown in communication. Friends and partners of people with Asperger syndrome need to communicate their feelings and emotions very clearly, and cannot assume that subtle changes in their tone of voice, facial expression or gestures will be noticed or understood.

Don't expect miraculous developments, but negotiate for change

Understanding that someone with Asperger syndrome has a particular style of interaction that is unlikely to change in any radical way is an important step towards developing functional relationships. However, discussion and negotiation between the parties to develop ground rules for the relationship, and finding simple techniques such as agreeing on routines, timetables and styles of communication, can all be helpful.

There are good reasons for apparently unreasonable behaviour

Appreciating that people with Asperger syndrome have a strong desire to follow familiar routines and to resist change makes it easier to understand their apparent lack of flexibility and spontaneity.

Avoid irony and sarcasm and be aware that teasing may not go down well

People with Asperger syndrome may be hypersensitive to innocuous comments made by other people. They may have difficulty coping with teasing, criticism or advice, or in understanding other people's sense of humour. Their literal interpretation of language can also cause difficulties if other people exaggerate or use sarcasm.

Recognise when a firm line needs to be drawn

It is not uncommon for people with Asperger syndrome to develop an intense special interest in another person. This involvement can take the form of amassing facts about a particular person, feeling possessive, becoming obsessed and can even extend into stalking behaviour.

Consider joint counselling for long-term, intimate relationships

If problems arise within long-term relationships, joint counselling from someone with knowledge of Asperger syndrome can be helpful. Some Relate counsellors have been given specialist training about Asperger syndrome and have been issued with guidance notes. The National Autistic Society (see Contact Addresses, p. 93) has a self-help register for partners and also publishes an information leaflet, 'Help for Partners of People with Asperger Syndrome'. Some regional offices of the NAS hold meetings for couples or for their partners on their own.

Conversation skills

Successful conversations require a number of different skills including attending, listening, contributing, giving others time to respond and turn-taking. All these skills can be challenging for people with Asperger syndrome, and even subtle difficulties can result in conversational breakdown. People's responses and reactions during conversations, both verbal and non-verbal, need to be observed and monitored continually to make certain that the exchange works and can be maintained.

Asking and answering questions is an accepted part of conversational turn-taking. It is important to let conversations develop naturally and to realise that they may evolve in unexpected directions. Conversations often falter when one party dominates, when there is much repetition or when the subject matter is very limited.

Conversational flow is enhanced when people show they have been paying attention by referring to what has been said in an earlier conversation. It can be helpful to remember particular things about people from previous meetings, such as where someone lives, what they are studying, their personal likes and dislikes or interests and to refer to this prior knowledge as a way of promoting good social interaction.

Sexuality

Because of their social difficulties, young people with Asperger syndrome tend to go through the potentially difficult period of puberty without being able to confide in others who are at the same age and stage. The onset of puberty and sexual awakening may develop later than average in people with Asperger syndrome, which also makes them feel different from their peer group. Intrinsic difficulties with social interaction and communication also affect the ability to engage in flirtatious or intimate interactions; this can result in feelings of sexual frustration and anxiety. A recent clinical study (Hénault 2003) indicates that 'the sexual profile of people with Asperger syndrome differs in several respects from that of the general population in relation to body image, sense of belonging to one's sex, and the erotic imagery of individuals with Asperger syndrome seems to be less influenced by social norms'.

There are a number of issues that people with Asperger syndrome and their partners need to acknowledge regarding dating and developing intimate relationships.

Sexual relationships are complex

Intimate relationships require advanced understanding of emotional states. Interpreting others' emotional states, such as happiness and anger, can be difficult enough, but sexual emotions are far more complicated and subtle. Specialist counselling or training that focuses on these more elusive emotions can be beneficial.

Flirtation can be hard to recognise

Individuals are not always aware when someone else is attracted to them or wishes to engage them in friendship. They may have difficulty reading flirtatious or teasing behaviour, which can lead to confusion and misunderstandings.

Flirting and dating have their own language, with gestures and rules that need to be explored and understood. Limited social interaction throughout the teenage years can make students appear naïve, inexperienced and lacking in self-confidence.

'It was only when I got a Valentine's card from a girl in my class that I realised she had fancied me for some time. I suddenly realised why she always seemed strange and awkward whenever I spoke to her. Until I got the card I didn't even know she liked me.' *EM*

Don't believe all you see in the media

Students' experience of sexuality may be limited to images in advertisements, television and film. These images often give an unrealistic and stereotypical impression, which, if they are taken literally or as role models, can be misleading, confusing and demoralising.

Make friends first

The confidence to be alone with another person and to feel comfortable in that situation needs to be established before any physical intimacy can be considered. Physical intimacy develops out of emotional intimacy and should be seen as a part of a close relationship. General training in social skills is a precursor to developing the more complex skills necessary for sexual interaction.

Be open

There is a close link between sexuality and the arousal of the senses. This can cause problems for those who are hyper-sensitive to sensory stimuli, particularly if there is an extreme response or aversion to touch or physical proximity. These problems need to be discussed openly and counselling sought if necessary.

Specialist counsellors attached to student support services or doctors' surgeries give advice on sexual problems, and also on birth control and sexual health.

Be aware of the possible effects of medication

Individuals who are taking antidepressant medication may experience side effects that lead to low sexual drive and erectile dysfunction.

The World Wide Web again

There are various books and internet resources that deal with intimate relationships and autistic spectrum disorders. See the section on Further Reading (p. 100) and Websites (pp. 98–99).

Electronic communication

Many people with Asperger syndrome find that relating to other people is much easier via electronic communication than face to face. They may use email, on-line newsletters, message boards or chat-rooms as a means of interaction. This can be a good way to share experiences with others without having to go through the intricacies of meeting people and developing personal relationships.

There are many websites dedicated to people with Asperger syndrome and this is often the only way that people have the opportunity to have contact with others who have faced similar difficulties and experiences.

> 'I gradually started talking to other people on the autistic spectrum via the Internet, which seems to be the ideal mode of communication for many of us, as it eliminates all the confusion and "overload" caused by body language, tone of voice, and other aspects of face-to-face interaction.' *Clare Sainsbury*

It is important to identify safe sites and to beware of confiding in others or giving too much personal information to strangers. 'Chatting' on email can make people feel less lonely and isolated and perhaps give them the opportunity to exchange ideas and make friends. Although electronic communication undoubtedly has its place, it is important to guard against it becoming an obsession, or used exclusively as a means of relating to others.

Bullying and social manipulation

Students with Asperger syndrome are vulnerable to bullying at college and university because of their difficulties with social interaction. Bullying is the assertion of power through aggression and can be physical, verbal or emotional. It can be direct, face to face or indirect, such as gossiping and exclusion. Bullying and manipulation by others can be very subtle and yet still cause great pain and distress to the recipient. Being ignored or ostracised from a group serves to increase feelings of isolation and loneliness. The desire to please and make friends can lead people with Asperger syndrome into situations where they are used or manipulated by others. Support workers and teaching staff need to be aware of this possibility and create opportunities for the student to confide any concerns. They will then need to take appropriate action to address the problem.

> 'One evening my flatmates and their friends got drunk and started shouting at me through my bedroom door. They called me names and banged on the door and just mocked me when I begged them to leave me alone.' *CH*

Key points from Chapter 6

- People with Asperger syndrome are not unemotional; they just have difficulty expressing their emotions

- There is more to be gained, in all aspects of social interaction, by the disclosure of a diagnosis of Asperger syndrome than by keeping quiet about it

- Most people with Asperger syndrome want to make friends and have a good social life

- Friendships are more likely to develop if communication problems are discussed openly

- Relationships with peers range from casual acquaintances to intimate friends – but to reach intimacy you have to go through all the preliminary stages of developing friendship

- Bullying should not be tolerated and should be reported to a member of staff as soon as possible

- The Internet is one means of communication, but it shouldn't be the only one

7

Secondary and Associated Problems

People with Asperger syndrome are acknowledged as being susceptible to mental health problems, in particular depression and anxiety. These problems are most likely to develop in late adolescence and young adult life. The clinical features of Asperger syndrome may mask subtle signs of mental instability which can lead to late diagnosis. An increase in psychiatric problems, such as extreme social withdrawal, obsessions and phobias may be difficult to recognise as the beginnings of a mental health problem. In addition, events that to others might not appear to be stressful can cause extreme distress for people with Asperger syndrome and increase their vulnerability to eating, sleep and attention disorders.

Depression

Students with Asperger syndrome are vulnerable to depression. Feelings of depression are likely to come to the fore at the time when young adults leave school and perhaps home for the first time. A precipitating factor is the major change to routine and lifestyle which can exacerbate existing feelings of insecurity and vulnerability. In addition, coming to terms with adult independence and responsibilities can highlight the full extent of their difficulties. People with Asperger syndrome can feel very

> 'My perception of reality began twisting itself into a convoluted mess, and so I plunged into my first year with a state of mind beleaguered with negative thoughts.' *EM*

isolated when surrounded by peers who appear to have no difficulty making friends. They may long to have a busy social life and to fit in with the crowd, but it just doesn't happen for them. The belief that they are different from others and that no one understands them can lead to loneliness, sadness, despair and even to self-loathing or self-harming.

The clinical symptoms of depression in an individual with Asperger syndrome are likely to be the same as in those without the condition. A diagnosis of depression will only be reached through consideration of a full case history, with account taken of established, long-standing behaviours.

Signs of depression include:

- mood swings
- loss of appetite
- sleep disturbance
- concentration problems
- memory loss
- preoccupation with death
- low motivation
- impaired social interaction

- exaggerated emotional responses
- changes in levels of activity
- aggressive behaviour.

Treatment

Treatment should initially address whether the origin of the depression is a reaction to specific events, such as loneliness, or fear of a new environment or situation. If the latter is the case, appropriate support, counselling and practical strategies may be enough to alleviate the symptoms of depression. Treatment with conventional medication may also be indicated. Students who think they might be suffering from depression should, in the first instance, make an appointment with their GP at the university health centre.

Anxiety

Anxiety is a normal aspect of behaviour and its manifestations are recognised universally. It is usually triggered by events that are widely acknowledged to cause anxiety – for example, examinations, speaking in public, being in a frightening or threatening situation or encountering a pet hate such as a spider or snake. Anxiety only becomes a problem when these feelings occur frequently or do not have an obvious cause. If anxiety is a pervasive problem it becomes a chronic, dominating force that can disrupt and interfere with daily functioning.

Tony Attwood (1998) states that 'many young adults with Asperger syndrome report intense feelings of anxiety, an anxiety that may reach a level where treatment is required. The person may develop panic attacks or compulsive behaviour such as having to wash their hands for fear of contamination.' People with Asperger syndrome are particularly prone to anxiety disorders because so many everyday situations can be extremely stressful and anxiety-provoking. Even apparently straightforward social exchanges or unfamiliar situations and activities can induce a high degree of anxiety.

Physiological changes take place in the body at times of anxiety because of increased adrenaline levels in the blood. These changes include:

- dizziness
- shortness of breath or shallow breathing
- nausea
- numbness
- shaking
- terror
- sweating
- increased heart rate
- muscle tension or weakness.

When these signs are recognised as indicators of an imminent anxiety attack it may be possible to prevent the onset of the attack by using strategies such as deep breathing, relaxation techniques or strenuous physical activity.

Anxiety can present in a number of different disorders. The most common are as follows.

Panic disorder

This disorder is characterised by spontaneous anxiety attacks without any obvious trigger. They typically last for about ten minutes. Treatment usually takes the form of cognitive behavioural therapy including relaxation and controlled breathing, or of medication. Often a combination of both types of treatment is the most effective. Between 70 and 90 per cent of sufferers are helped by these approaches.

Specific phobias

A phobia is an extreme fear of particular objects, activities or situations. Phobias are very common, affecting more than one in ten people in the general population. Individuals with Asperger syndrome often have agoraphobia (from the Greek 'agora' meaning market) – a fear of leaving a specified safety zone. This phobia responds to both therapeutic and medical treatment. Other phobias respond best to desensitisation or exposure therapy, or relaxation and breathing techniques rather than medication.

Generalised anxiety disorder

This produces a constant and extreme feeling of nervousness, tension or fear in the absence of any evident provoking factors. For example, someone who has spent at least six months worrying excessively about an apparently trivial issue might be diagnosed as having generalised anxiety disorder. The symptoms usually become less acute with age and experience. Treatment takes the form of cognitive behaviour therapy including relaxation and breathing techniques.

Social anxiety

As the name suggests, social anxiety is a fear of interacting with other people. This is a common condition affecting approximately 7 per cent of the population at some time in their lives. People with Asperger syndrome are particularly vulnerable to this condition as it is an extreme form of their existing social difficulties. Social anxiety is an excessive form of shyness which interferes with day-to-day living.

Confidence and assertiveness training, counselling, mentoring and befriending schemes are all used to help people cope with this type of anxiety.

Obsessive compulsive disorder

Obsessive compulsive disorder (OCD) is a condition characterised by recurring, obsessive thoughts (obsessions) or compulsive actions (compulsions). Obsessive thoughts are ideas, pictures of thoughts or impulses which can repeatedly enter the mind, whereas compulsive actions and rituals are behaviours which are repeated over and over again. People suffering with OCD are frequently plagued by repetitive or disturbing thoughts or images, or the need to perform certain rituals. These rituals may be related to washing, checking and counting, or touching. Carrying out these rituals does not provide any comfort or pleasure; there is simply a powerful, uncontrollable force from within to continue to perform them.

Obsessions and compulsions are a recognised feature of Asperger syndrome related to inflexibility of thought. As with other psychiatric disorders, it can be difficult to differentiate between Asperger-type obsessions and obsessive compulsive disorder.

Treatment for obsessions and compulsions is only effective if the individual is highly motivated to control the disorder. Cognitive behavioural therapy is often successful. In this form of treatment the patient is exposed to the event that triggers an obsession or compulsion, and is then helped to avoid going through the associated ritual. Alternatively, medication has a role in reducing obsessions and compulsions, and medication may be used in conjunction with therapy.

Attention Deficit Disorder (ADD) and Attention Deficit Hyperactivity Disorder (ADHD)

Problems with attention are often associated with Asperger syndrome. Occasionally in addition to attention deficits there is over-activity and impulsivity as well. When people with Asperger syndrome have ADD they will frequently appear to be absorbed in their own thoughts or activities rather than attending to what is happening in their immediate environment. They can thus appear to be very easily distracted, but their attention deficit may take a subtly different form from that observed in people who have ADD without Asperger syndrome. Recent research (Eisenmajer *et al.* 1996) suggests that one in six individuals with Asperger syndrome show the characteristic signs of ADD (or ADHD). This dual diagnosis needs appropriate management and, where indicated, treatment with medication.

Tics and Tourette syndrome

Tics – involuntary muscular movements – are commonly seen in people with Asperger syndrome at some time in their lives. There is also evidence that the prevalence of Tourette syndrome in people with Asperger syndrome is much higher than in the general population, perhaps as high as one in ten. Tourette syndrome is characterised by motor tics, vocal outbursts and behavioural signs. Involuntary motor tics can take the form of excessive or exaggerated eye blinking, facial grimacing and head or limb movements. Vocal outbursts can take the form of throat clearing, barking, shrieking, yelping, repeating what someone has just said (echolalia), and occasionally shouting obscenities for no apparent reason. The behavioural signs of Tourette syndrome are often of an obsessive or compulsive nature, such as checking, counting or touching. A combination of medication and cognitive behavioural therapy can be effective.

Alcohol and drug abuse

The fact that some people with Asperger syndrome have some immunity to peer pressure can mean that they are less likely to follow the crowd and participate in excessive bouts of drinking as students. For this reason they may also be less likely to experiment with drugs. However, alcohol can be seen as a way of dealing with stressful situations, of compensating for loneliness or of escaping from difficulties, so there is a risk of developing a drink problem. Recent studies (cited by Gillberg 2002) have shown that the rate of alcohol abuse may be very high in people with Asperger syndrome. There is no clear research to indicate that drug experimentation is any higher in people with Asperger syndrome than in the general population. It is important to remember that anyone with high levels of anxiety and a predisposition to mental and emotional disturbances is at much greater risk of experiencing extreme reactions to alcohol or drugs, in particular episodes of paranoia.

Support and counselling about the effects of substance abuse on general health and the problems of side effects can often be convincing enough to encourage people with Asperger syndrome to avoid becoming dependent on alcohol or drugs.

Eating disorders

Some children with Asperger syndrome have very limited and repetitive eating patterns. These problems may become more pronounced during adolescence and develop into a recognised eating disorder such as anorexia nervosa. Diet may be limited to a few foods that are eaten at every meal. Occasionally the diet is so restricted that only certain brands of a particular food will be eaten. This has both social and nutritional implications. Some people are not conscious of feeling either hungry or thirsty and need to be reminded when it is time to eat or drink. There is no evidence that the eating disorder bulimia nervosa, where binge eating and vomiting occurs, is seen any more commonly in people with Asperger syndrome than in the general population. Treatment of these problems includes education about nutrition and healthy eating regimes, but if eating problems interfere seriously with day-to-day life, medical or therapeutic intervention may be required.

Sleep disorders

Sleep may become disrupted or disordered in people with Asperger syndrome, particularly at stressful times. Abnormal sleep patterns are often seen in children and these patterns often become more acute during adolescence. Difficulty getting to sleep, frequent waking throughout the night and problems with either early waking or difficulty getting up in the morning are problems experienced by many teenagers, but they appear to become more acute for young adults with Asperger syndrome. Sleep disturbance can be helped by regular sleep times, bedtime routines, and by relaxation and breathing techniques.

Key points from Chapter 7

- Students with Asperger syndrome are vulnerable to a range of mental health problems

- Personal tutors who recognise that students may be at risk should advise them to see their GP or to contact the student counselling service

- Anxiety can be termed a disorder if it interferes with normal daily functioning

- Relaxation and breathing techniques are effective in treating anxiety and sleep disorders

- A combination of cognitive behavioural therapy and medication is often useful in treating mental health problems

- Students with Asperger syndrome often have difficulty sustaining expected levels of attention

RESOURCES

CD and Resources for Photocopying

This section of the book contains a number of resources that have been developed to be used by students themselves or their support workers.

These resources can be photocopied directly from the book or can be down-loaded onto a computer using the compact disc. The templates can be personalised for use by individuals or the institution concerned.

1. Advance information for interview panel

This sheet can be sent to an interview panel when the student confirms that he or she will be attending an interview. It can be personalised for each student by deleting or adding to the proforma.

2. General information leaflet for academic staff

This information sheet can be personalised for an individual student by deleting or adding to the proforma. The student should agree to any changes that are made and then, with their permission, it can be circulated to teaching staff.

3. Initial interview

This interview form can be used by disability assessors, mentors or personal tutors to provide an individual profile on a student. From the information gathered in this interview it should be possible to isolate specific areas of need and concern, which can then be addressed by the provision of appropriate support. The interview takes between one and two hours to complete, so it may be necessary to conduct it in two separate sessions. The detailed interview structure can be downloaded from the accompanying CD.

4. Mentoring record form

This form can be used for structuring a mentoring session. It forms a useful record of the sessions and is a helpful method of documenting and monitoring progress.

5. Individual student proforma for course staff or personal tutors

This sheet can be used as a template and personalised for individual students. It is divided into two parts: the effects Asperger syndrome has on the student's social and learning skills, and recommended departmental support. Any factors that do not apply to a specific student can be deleted. The page has a small font size to enable all the information to be on one page; the font size can be increased accordingly once the relevant deletions have been made.

6. Weekly timetable

This is a simple grid showing the all hours between 7 a.m. and midnight for each day of the week. It can be printed off weekly or in advance to help students to plan their time for study, leisure and domestic activities.

Advance Information for Interview Panel

_____ has been invited to attend an interview at

_____ on _____ .

_____ has a diagnosis of Asperger syndrome which affects social skills and interaction. In an interview the following difficulties may arise:

- ☐ maintaining appropriate eye contact

- ☐ appropriate use of tone or volume of voice

- ☐ aspects of verbal comprehension, including inference and understanding idioms or sarcasm

- ☐ addressing more than one person on the interview panel

- ☐ knowing how much to say

- ☐ changing from one subject to another

- ☐ taking account of the panel's prior knowledge (or lack thereof)

- ☐ interpreting feedback signals from the panel

- ☐ anticipating when the interview is coming to an end

- ☐ leaving the room at the end of the interview

It would be very helpful for all members of the interview panel to be given this information in advance and for these factors to be taken into consideration.

General Information Leaflet

Disability Co-ordinator:

Student Support Services:

Asperger Syndrome

Information for University and College Teaching Staff

Asperger syndrome is a pervasive developmental disorder on the autism spectrum. Approximately one person in every 300 has this condition, which is much more prevalent in males than in females. Although the condition is not new, it has been relatively recently identified, and it is only in the last 15 to 20 years that diagnoses have been regularly made in Britain. People with Asperger syndrome are of normal intelligence and many are academically gifted.

Asperger syndrome is characterised by difficulties in the following three areas:

Social Interaction

Severe impairment in reciprocal social interaction

Desire to make friends but has difficulty achieving this

Difficulty seeing things from another's perspective

Difficulty interpreting people's intentions

Language and Communication

Unusual style of speech and language

Literal interpretation of language

Unusual eye contact and other non-verbal communication

Difficulty describing feelings and emotions

Rigidity and Inflexibility

All-absorbing narrow interests and/or obsessions

Imposition of rituals, routines and interests, on self and others

Resistance to change

Students with Asperger syndrome face many challenges at university. Tutors may find, for example, that they do not work well in groups, need very explicit instructions and feedback and have difficulty organising their time. With appropriate support their ability to reach their academic potential can be maximised.

Initial interview

There is a structured interview form provided on the accompanying CD. This can be printed out and used by tutors to explore with students the types of difficulties they may encounter at college or university and what kind of support will be most appropriate

Mentoring Sessions – Record Form

A suggested structure for mentoring sessions is provided below. The accompanying CD contains the same text in interview format, i.e. with spaces in which responses can be written.

Mentoring Sessions

☐ Weekly

☐ Fortnightly

☐ Monthly

Name of student: _____

Name of mentor: _____

Date: _____

Date of previous session: _____

Session number: _____

Venue: _____

General discussion (issues that have arisen since previous session):

_____

Specific experiences or events that have been either positive or negative:

_____

Can anything be learnt from these experiences?

_____

Are there any specific strategies, changes or adaptations that can be implemented to help learn and generalise from these experiences?

_____

Specific targets for the period between now and the next mentoring session:

_____

Other issues or topics discussed:

_____

Date, time and venue for next session:

_____

Confidential Information for Academic Staff

Student's name: _____

Department: _____Tutor:_____

Course and Year _____

_____ has a diagnosis of Asperger syndrome, and has given permission for this information to be passed on to you, as the personal tutor, and to lectures and tutors in your department.

_____ has difficulty with:

☐ social interaction

☐ social understanding

☐ certain aspects of language comprehension

☐ working in a group

☐ motor skills including handwriting

☐ adapting to change

☐ sustaining concentration

☐ managing stress

☐ time management

☐ organisational skills

Recommended departmental support:

☐ Access to a mentor and a named member of staff available to offer support

☐ Permission to use a mini-disk or Dictaphone to record key parts of lectures, seminars and tutorials

☐ Sensitive introduction to group activities, monitoring and addressing problems that arise

☐ Provision of handouts or overheads in advance of lectures when possible

☐ Opportunity to use a laptop computer

☐ Preparation and support offered at times of change such as exams, reading weeks or field trips

☐ Clear timetables and, where possible, advanced notice of any timetable changes

☐ Opportunity to leave the room at times of stress and access to a safe area

Student's signature: _____ Date: _____

Staff signature: _____ Role: _____

WEEKLY TIMETABLE for week beginning:

Time Date	Monday	Tuesday	Wednesday	Thursday	Friday	Saturday	Sunday
7–8							
8–9							
9–10							
10–11							
11–12							
12–1							
1–2							
2–3							
3–4							
4–5							
5–6							
6–7							
7–8							
8–9							
9–10							
10–11							
11–12							

- breakfast, lunch, dinner, shower, laundry, cleaning, paying bills, shopping
- lectures, tutorials, private study, hand-in dates for coursework
- clubs, societies, sports, cinema

References

American Psychiatric Association (1994) *Diagnostic and Statistical Manual of Mental Disorders (DSM-IV),* 4th edn. Washington, DC: APA.

Asperger, H. (1944) 'Die Autistischen Psychopathen', *Kindesalter, Archiv. fur Psychiatrie und Nervenkrankheiten*, 117, 76–136.

Asperger, H. (1979) 'Problems of infantile autism', *Communication* 13, 45–52.

Attwood, T. (1998) *Asperger's Syndrome: A Guide for Parents and Professionals.* London: Jessica Kingsley Publishers.

Baron-Cohen, S., Leslie, A. M. and Frith, U. (1985) 'Does the autistic child have a "theory of mind"?' *Cognition* 21, 37–46.

Buzan, T. (1974) *Use Your Head.* London: BBC Books.

Eisenmajer, R., Prior, M., Leekman, S., Wing, L., Gould, J., Welham, M. and Ong, B. (1996) 'Comparisons of clinical symptoms in autism and Asperger's syndrome', *Journal of the American Academy of Child and Adolescent Psychiatry*, 35, 1523–31.

Frith, U. (1991) 'Asperger and his syndrome', in U. Frith (ed.) *Autism and Asperger Syndrome.* Cambridge: Cambridge University Press.

Frith, U. (2003) 'Brain and mind in Asperger syndrome: Summary of the 2002 Emanuel Lecture'. Interventions for individuals with Asperger's Syndrome. London: Association for Child Psychology and Psychiatry, Occasional papers No. 21.

Gillberg, C. (1991) 'Clinical and neurobiological aspects of Asperger syndrome in six family studies', in U. Frith (ed.) *Autism and Asperger Syndrome.* Cambridge: Cambridge University Press.

Gillberg, C. (2002) *A Guide to Asperger Syndrome.* Cambridge: Cambridge University Press.

Gillberg, C. and Gillberg, I. C. (1989) 'Asperger syndrome – some epidemiological considerations: A research note', *Journal of Child Psychology and Psychiatry*, 30, 631–8.

Harrison, J. and Baron-Cohen, S. (1995) 'Synaesthesia: reconciling the subjective with the objective', *Endeavour*, 19, 157–60.

Hénault, I. (2003) 'The sexuality of adolescents with Asperger syndrome', in L. Holliday Willey (ed.) *Asperger Syndrome in Adolescence – Living with the Ups, the Downs and the Things in Between.* London: Jessica Kingsley Publishers.

Holliday Willey, L. (1999) *Pretending to be Normal – Living with Asperger's Syndrome.* London: Jessica Kingsley Publishers.

Howlin, P. (1997) *Autism: Preparing for Adulthood.* London: Routledge.

Jackson, L. (2002) *Freaks, Geeks & Asperger syndrome – A User Guide to Adolescence.* London: Jessica Kingsley Publishers.

Rimland, B. (1990) 'Sound sensitivity in autism', *Autism Research Review International*, 4, 1 and 6.

Sacks, O. (1995) 'Musical ability' (Letter), *Science*, 268, 621.

Sainsbury, C. (2000) *Martian in the Playground*. Bristol: Lucky Duck Publishing Ltd.

Tantum, D. (1991) 'Asperger's syndrome in adulthood', in U. Frith (ed.) *Autism and Asperger's Syndrome*. Cambridge: Cambridge University Press.

WHO (1993) *The ICD-10 Classification of Mental and Behavioural Disorders: Diagnostic Criteria for Research*. Geneva: World Health Organisation.

Williams, D. (1994) *Somebody Somewhere*. London: Transworld.

Wing, L. (1981) 'Asperger syndrome: a clinical account', *Psychological Medicine*, **11**, 115–30.

Wing, L. (1988) 'The continuum of autistic characteristics', in F. Shopler and G. B. Mesibov (eds) *Diagnosis and Assessment in Autism*. New York: Plenum Press.

Contact Addresses and Resources

Organisations

Connexions
Tel: +44 (0)8080 013219
Textphone: +44 (0)7766 413219
Connexions Direct: www.connexions-direct.com

Department for Education and Skills (DfES)
Sanctury Buildings
Great Smith Street
London SW1P 3BT
Information freephone: 0800 731 9133
www.dfes.gov.uk

The DSA comes under the remit of the DfES; information from
www.dfes.gov.uk/studentsupport

ESPA (European Services for People with Autism)
Ashleigh College
3 Elmfield Park
Gosforth
Newcastle upon Tyne NE3 4UX
Tel: +44 (0)191 213 0833

A registered charity offering services to people from all over the UK.

Glasgow College of Nautical Studies
21 Thistle Street
Glasgow G5 9XB
Tel: +44 (0)141 565 2500
Email: enquiries@gcns.ac.uk

InterACT Centre
c/o The Acton Centre
Mill Hill Road
London W3 8UX
Tel: +44 (0)20 8896 1911
Email: office@theinteractcentre.com
www.theinteractcentre.com

An educational resource centre in London for young people with Asperger syndrome.

The National Autistic Society
393 City Road
London EC1V 1NG
Tel: +44 (0)20 7833 2299
Fax: +44 (0)20 7833 9666
Email: nas@nas.org.uk

The National Autistic Society, Wales
Suite C1, William Knox House
Britannic Way
Llandarcy
Neath
West Glamorgan SA10 6EL
Tel: +44 (0)1792 815915
www.nas.org.uk

NAS Family Service Workers
Offers support to adults. Contact the Manchester Branch of the NAS:
Tel: +44 (0)161 998 4667

National Federation of Access Centres (NFAC)
The Administrative Centre
Disability Assist Services
University of Plymouth
Drake Circus
Plymouth PL4 8AA
Tel: +44 (0)1752 232278
Email: das@plymouth.ac.uk
www.nfac.org.uk

National Mentoring Network
First Floor, Charles House
Albert Street
Eccles M30 0PD
Tel: +44 (0)161 787 8600
Fax: +44 (0)161 787 8100
Email: enquiries@nmn.org.uk

Northern Ireland
Students' Awards
Belfast Education and Library Board
40 Academy Street
Belfast BT1 2NQ
Tel: +44 (0)28 9056 4237/8
Email: student.awards@belb.co.uk
www.belb.org.uk

The Open University
Walton Hall
Milton Keynes MK7 6ZN
Tel: +44 (0)1908 654136
Textphone: +44 (0)1908 659955
Fax: +44 (0)1908 659956
Email: general_enquiries@open.ac.uk

The Open University Scotland
10 Drumsheugh Gardens
Edinburgh EH12 9HH
Tel: +44 (0)131 226 3851
Email: Scotland@open.ac.uk

The Oxford Stress and Trauma Centre
8a Market Square
Witney OX28 6BB
Tel: +44 (0)1993 779077
Fax: +44 (0)1993 779499
www.oxfdev.co.uk

Part of the Oxford Development Centre Ltd. The Centre provides assessment and treatment of trauma and stress-related problems and has a mail order book service.

Prospects
An employment consultancy set up by the NAS with regional offices.

London:
Tel: +44 (0)20 7704 7450
Email: Prospects-London@nas.org.uk

Glasgow:
Tel: +44 (0)141 248 1725
Email: Prospects-Glasgow@nas.org.uk

Manchester:
Tel: +44 (0)161 998 0577
Email: ruthblackledge@nas.org.uk

Sheffield:
Tel: +44 (0)114 225 5695
Email: dlarman@nas.org.uk

Relate
Helpline: +44 (0)1332 345678
Relate in Derby offers counselling to adults with Asperger syndrome, or their partners. The helpline is open every Tuesday 10.30–4.30 and helps people from all over the UK.

SKILL
National Bureau for Students with Disabilities

Chapter House
18–20 Crucifix Lane
London SE1 3JW
Skill Information Service Tel: 0800 328 5050
www.skill.org.uk

SKILL promotes opportunities for young people and adults with any kind of disability in post-16 education, training and employment across the UK. The organisation offers an information service for disabled people, their families or people working with them, publishing books, booklets and leaflets, including one titled 'Disabled Students' Allowance'.

Students Awards Agency for Scotland (SAAS)
Gyleview House
3 Redheughs Rigg
Edinburgh EH12 9HH
Tel: +44 (0)845 111 0244
Email: saas.geu@scotland.gsi.gov
www.saas.gov.uk

Student Loans Company Ltd
100 Bothwell Street
Glasgow G2 7JD
Tel: +44 (0)800 405010

UCAS
Rosehill
New Barn Lane
Cheltenham GL52 3LZ
Tel: +44 (0)1242 223707

Assessment and Diagnosis

Autism Independent UK
199–205 Blandford Avenue
Kettering
Northamptonshire NN16 9AT
Tel: +44 (0)1536 523 274
www.autismuk.com

The Centre for Social and Communication Disorders
Elliot House
113 Masons Hill
Bromley
Kent BR2 9HT

Tel: +44 (0)20 8466 0098
Fax: +44 (0)20 84660118
Email: elliot.house@nas.org.uk

CLASS (Cambridge Lifespan Asperger Syndrome Service)
Department of Experimental Psychology
University of Cambridge
Downing Street
Cambridge CB2 3EB
Tel: +44 (0)1223 333557

Dilemma Consultancy in Human Relations
27 Brocco Bank
Sheffield S11 8RQ
Tel: +44 (0)114 230 9990

Hoffman de Visme Foundation
Asperger Service
Unit B
Lynton Road
Crouch End
London N8 8SL
Tel: +44 (0)20 8342 7310

The Maudsley Centre for Behavioural Disorders
Bethlem Royal Hospital
Beckenham
Kent SE5 8AZ
Tel: +44 (0)20 8776 4696

Publishers

Blue Stallion Publications
(Part of the Oxford Development Centre – see the Oxford Stress and Trauma Centre under
Organisations)
www.blue-stallion.co.uk

David Fulton Publishers
The Chiswick Centre
414 Chiswick High Road
London W4 5TF
Tel: +44 (0)20 8996 3610
Fax: +44 (0)20 8996 3622
Email: mail@fultonpublishers.co.uk

Jessica Kingsley Publishers
116 Pentonville Road
London N1 9JB
Tel: +44 (0)20 7833 2307
Email: post@jkp.com
www.jkp.com

Lucky Duck Publishing Ltd
3 Thorndale Mews
Clifton
Bristol BS8 2HX
Tel: +44 (0)117 973 2881
Fax: +44 (0)117 973 1707
Email: publishing@luckyduck.co.uk

The National Autistic Society
HO Publications Department
Tel: +44 (0)20 7903 3595
NAS books can be ordered through Barnardos Dispatch Services:
Tel: +44 (0)1268 522872
Fax: +44 (0)1268 284804
Email: Beverley.bennett@barnardos.org.uk

PRO-ED
8700 Shoal Creek Boulevard
Austin
Texas
TX 78757
USA

Websites

Website listing clinicians who diagnose Asperger syndrome
www.aspergers.com/asplist.htm

OASIS (On-line Asperger Syndrome Information Service)
OASIS is an American website with links to many other websites.
www.aspergersyndrome.org

Aspiechat IRC channel
www.geocities.com/RainForest/Jungle/2223/aspiechat.html
aspiechat@hotmail.com

Autism Network International
A website where other people with Asperger syndrome can be contacted online via email.
www.students.uiuc.edu/~border/ani.html

Families of Adults Afflicted with Asperger Syndrome (FAAAS)
Information for partners and spouses of individuals with Asperger syndrome.
www.faaas.org/

Independent living on the autistic spectrum (InLv)
Contains many articles and links related to independent living.
www.inlv.demon.nl

University Students with Autism and Asperger Syndrome
http://www.users.dircon.co.uk/~cns/

Tony Attwood's homepage
Plenty of information about Asperger syndrome.
http://www.tonyattwood.com.au/

Oops . . . Wrong Planet Syndrome
http://www.isn.net/~jypsy/

Obsessive Compulsive Disorder Foundation website
www.ocfoundation.org/

Dyspraxia Foundation website
www.dyspraxiafoundation.org.uk/

Student Counselling
Lists addresses and telephone numbers of student counselling services throughout the UK.
www.studentcounselling.org/index

Intimate Relationships
www.autismuk.com/index9sub.html

Gap Year
www.gap-year.com
www.yearoutgroup.org/index.html
www.schoolzone.co.uk/students/exams/Gapyear.htm
http://www.ceg.org.uk/general/Taking+a+Gap+Year.htm

Further reading

Aston, M. C. (2001) *The Other Half of Asperger Syndrome.* London: The National Autistic Society.

Attwood, T. (1989) *Asperger's Syndrome: A Guide for Parents and Professionals.* London: Jessica Kingsley Publishers.

Attwood, T. (1993) *Why Does Chris Do That? Some suggestions regarding the cause and management of the unusual behaviour of children and adults with autism and Asperger syndrome.* London: The National Autistic Society.

Baron-Cohen, S. (1995) *Mindblindness: An Essay on Autism and Theory of Mind.* Cambridge, Mass: MIT Press.

Baron-Cohen, S. and Bolton, P. (1993) *Autism: the Facts.* Oxford: Oxford University Press.

Baron-Cohen, S., Tager-Flusburg, H. and Cohen, D. (eds) (1999) *Understanding Other Minds: Perspectives from Autism.* Oxford: Oxford University Press.

Bicknell, A. (1999) *Independent Living for Adults with Autism and Asperger Syndrome. A guide for families of people with autistic spectrum disorders.* London: The National Autistic Society.

Brown, A. and Miller, A. (2003) *Aspects of Asperger's – Success in the teens and twenties.* Bristol: Lucky Duck Publishing Ltd.

Cumine, V., Leach, J. and Stevenson, G. (1998) *Asperger's Syndrome: A Practical Guide for Teachers.* London: David Fulton Publishers Ltd.

Frith, U. (1989) *Autism: Explaining the Enigma.* Oxford: Basil Blackwell.

Frith, U. (1991) *Autism and Asperger's Syndrome.* Cambridge: Cambridge University Press.

Fullerton, A., Stratton, J., Coyne, P. and Gray, C. (1996) *Higher Functioning Adolescents and Young Adults with Autism: A Teacher's Guide.* Austin, Tex: Pro-ed.

Gabor, D. (1983) *How to Start a Conversation and Make Friends.* London: Sheldon Press.

Gillberg, C. (2002) *A Guide to Asperger Syndrome.* Cambridge: Cambridge University Press.

Gillberg, C. and Coleman, M. (2000) *The Biology of the Autistic Syndromes.* 3rd edn. Antwerp: Whurr Publishers.

Grandin, T. (1992) 'An Inside View of Autism', in E. Schopler and G. B. Mesibov (eds) *High Functioning Individuals with Autism.* New York: Plenum Press.

Grandid, T. (1996) *Thinking in Pictures and Other Reports of My Life with Autism.* New York: Vintage Books.

Gray, S., Ruble, L. and Dalrymple, N. (1996) *Autism and Sexuality: A Guide for Instruction.* Bloomington, Ind: Autism Society of Indiana.

Holliday Willey, L. (2000) *Pretending to be Normal.* London: Jessica Kingsley Publishers.

Howlin, P. (1997) *Autism: Preparing for Adulthood.* London: Routledge.

Jordan, R. (1999) *Autistic Spectrum Disorders: An Introductory Handbook for Practitioners.* London: David Fulton Publishers.

Kanner, L. (1943) 'Autistic disturbances of affective contact', *Nervous Child*, 2, 217–50.

Kempton, W. (1993) 'Socialisation and Sexuality: A Comprehensive Training Guide', *Journal of Autism and Developmental Disorders*, 27, 2.

Le Breton, M. (2001) *Diet Intervention and Autism: Implementing the Gluten Free and Casein Free Diet for Autistic Children and Adults.* London: Jessica Kingsley Publishers.

Mawhood, L. and Howlin, P. (1997) *A Supported Employment Scheme for Able Adults with Autism or Asperger Syndrome.* London: The National Autistic Society.

Rinaldi, W. (2001) *Social Use of Language Programme* (SULP) (rev. edn). Windsor: NFER Nelson.

Sainsbury, C. (2000) *Martian in the Playground.* Bristol: Lucky Duck Publishing Ltd.

Schopler, E. and Mesibov, G. B. (ed.) (1992) *High Functioning Individuals with Autism.* New York: Plenum Press.

Schopler, E., Mesibov, G. B. and Kunce, L. J. (eds) (1998) *Asperger Syndrome or High Functioning Autism?* New York: Plenum Press.

Tantum, D. (1991) *A Mind of One's Own: A guide to the special difficulties of the more able person with autism, for parents, professionals and people with autism* (2nd edn). London: The National Autistic Society.

Tantum, D. (1991) 'Asperger syndrome in adulthood', in U. Frith (ed.) *Autism and Asperger Syndrome.* Cambridge: Cambridge University Press.

Tantum, D. and Prestwood, S. (1988) *A Mind of One's Own – A guide to the special needs and difficulties of the more able person with autism or Asperger syndrome.* London: The National Autistic Society.

Taylor, G. (1990) 'Adolescence and early adulthood', in K. Ellis (ed.) *Autism: Professional Perspectives and Practice.* London: Chapman and Hall.

Tipper, M. (2002) *The Positively Mad Guide to the Secrets of Successful Students.* Bristol: Lucky Duck Publishing Ltd.

Treffert, D. (1989) *Extraordinary People.* London: Bantam Press.

Williams, D. (1992) *Nobody Nowhere.* London: Transworld/Doubleday.

Williams, D. (1996) *Autism, An Inside-out Approach.* London: Jessica Kingsley Publishers.

Williams, D. (1999) *Like Colour to the Blind: Soul Searching and Soul Finding.* London: Jessica Kingsley Publishers.

Wing, L. (1996) *The Autism Spectrum: A Guide for Parents and Professionals.* London: Constable.

Journals

Autism: the International Journal of Research and Practice
Journal of the National Autistic Society.
SAGE Publications Ltd
1 Oliver's Yard
55 City Road
London EC1Y 1SP
Tel: +44 (0)20 7324 8500
Email: subscription@sagepub.co.uk

Communication
Published three times a year by the National Autistic Society. Available to members only.

Titles in Autism
Published three times a year by the National Autistic Society.

Good Autism Practice
Promotes good practice for child and adult services for people with autism spectrum disorders.
Published bi-annually.
BILD
Wolverhampton Road
Kidderminster

Worcester DY10 3PP
Tel: +44 (0)1562 850251
Email: LesBrown@bild-irc.demon.co.uk

Journal of Autism and Developmental Disorders
Published six times a year.
Plenum Publishing Corporation
233 Spring Street
New York
NY 10013
USA
Tel: +1 212 620 8468/70/72

Link Bulletin
Published quarterly.
Autism Europe
Rue E. Van Becelaere 26B
Bte 21
B-1170
Brussels
Belgium

Looking Up
Newsletter covering international issues related to autism spectrum disorders.
PO Box 25727
London SW19 1WF
Tel/Fax: +44 (0) 20 8542 7702
Email: 100675.1146@compuserve.com

Index